CUSTOMERS
FIRST

DOMINATE YOUR MARKET
BY WINNING THEM OVER
WHERE IT COUNTS THE MOST

BOLIVAR J. BUENO

New York Chicago San Francisco Lisbon London Madrid Mexico City
Milan New Delhi San Juan Seoul Singapore Sydney Toronto

1 2 3 4 5 6 7 8 9 10 DOC/DOC 1 8 7 6 5 4 3 2

ISBN   978-0-07-178787-1
MHID   0-07-178787-9

e-ISBN   978-0-07-178788-8
e-MHID   0-07-178788-7

Library of Congress Cataloging-in-Publication Data

Bueno, Bolivar J.
    Customers first : dominate your market by winning them over where it counts the most / by Bolivar J. Bueno.
    p. cm.
ISBN 978-0-07-178787-1 (alk. paper) — ISBN 0-07-178787-9 (alk. paper)
1. Branding (Marketing). 2. Customer relations. 3. Brand name products. I. Title.
HF5415.1255.B84 2012
658.8'12—dc23

                                                                        2011048925

McGraw-Hill books are available at special quantity discounts to use as premiums and sales promotions or for use in corporate training programs. To contact a representative, please e-mail us at bulksales@mcgraw-hill.com.

This book is printed on acid-free paper.

Contents

FOREWORD

Every journey requires some kind of compass—a sense of where one is headed and an assurance that one is on the right path.

This book is, in a word, a compass.

As a marketer, keeping the brand that I steward on track is perhaps the most important and difficult challenge I face daily. The rate of speed at which the world is changing requires significant insights, strategies, and nimbleness. Today's environment can be a destroyer of brands if one is not consistently in tune with the customer.

Having a Brand Model based on insights into one's customers is invaluable. Even better is having a customer-focused model that is dimensionalized so that one can use it as a guide to assess potential scenarios and strategies, allowing for a fluid yet disciplined approach that will grow the brand instead of diluting it.

BJ's Brand Modeling process provides a deep understanding of the passion that one's best customers have for the brands they love. This understanding guides the strategies and dialogue within the organization with confidence and alignment that expedites decisions and provides the filter through which decisions are made and positive results are achieved.

I've been a marketer on the agency and client side for more than 20 years. There are two key brand killers that are always at your doorstep: apathy and ideation. You can probably understand why apathy kills a brand (through a lack of energy), but you may wonder why I say that ideas can also kill a brand. After all, we are in the business of creating ideas, aren't we? The problem is that we often fall in love with ideas without properly evaluating whether these ideas are right for the brand. And since the customer defines the brand, ultimately the question that we must ask is, "Is it right for our best customers—our Brand Lovers?" To answer this question successfully, you must first understand the psychological makeup of your best customers. A customer-centric Brand Model helps you do just that.

Marketing is a delicate combination of art and science. The art is a beautiful flow of intangible emotions that connects brands and customers in a way that speaks to the customer's heart. The science of marketing can be elusive. A solid Brand Model uses customer insights to identify a brand's various dimensions based on evidence and facts. These verifiable data are undeniably insightful not only for the marketer, but for the entire organization, and they keep an organization from apathy and from falling in love with ideas that don't fit the brand.

Peter Drucker said that the best way to predict the future is to create it. I believe that the best way to predict the future of your brand is to acquire an in-depth understanding of your best customers and to use that knowledge to predict the future. Your best customers know the most about your brand; they love you and hold you to high standards. Understanding that love and using it to grow more customers is what BJ's Brand Modeling process is designed to do.

In *Customers First*, BJ makes a compelling case not only for Brand Modeling, but for the best approach to building a model, creating a strong and sustainable compass not only for marketers, but for the entire organization as well.

Julie Gardner
Chief Marketing Officer
Kohls Department Stores

PART I

Introduction:
Things Have Changed

CHAPTER 1

What You Don't Know Can Hurt You

Customers are skeptical. They've been lied to by just about everyone who's had the opportunity to do so. From role models who can't keep extramarital affairs from wrecking their golf game to behemoth corporations betting against their own customers' investments to politicians regularly resigning for engaging in the very activities they legislated against, no one has been telling the truth. You need an element of trust to get genuine customer buy-in, but we've spent a generation and a half teaching the public to trust nobody.

This creates a problem for today's business leaders. How do you connect with these empowered, educated, skeptical consumers? This is a question of some urgency. If you don't have the answer, you have to figure it out now, and you have to keep your business thriving at the same time. There's absolutely no time to hesitate. If you cannot connect with your customers in a meaningful way, you will become irrelevant to them. When you're irrelevant, you're replaceable, and your customers will inevitably replace you with a brand that they do feel connected to.

Irrelevancy arrives in those still moments when an organization is facing uncertainty. These are the times when the company is trying to figure out what to do. Choosing the right course is difficult: if you opt for the wrong direction, you'll saddle your company with the burden of invisibility when you're least prepared to bear it.

Let us show you how that happens.

Do You Want Fries with That?

Initially modeled on European cafés, Starbucks had a good thing going. We find Starbucks absolutely fascinating as a company. At the beginning, it made some excellent decisions from a brand-building perspective: Starbucks became a strong, and arguably an iconic, brand. Yet in the wake of this success came a series of inexplicably bad decisions that could imperil the brand's dominant position.

Starbucks captured its initial fan base by offering an experience unlike any other that was commonly available in America at the time. Customers responded to and valued the fact that Starbucks offered a unique experience. Starbucks's interpretation of the coffeehouse as a comfortable, upscale "third place" where customers could relax, self-actualize, and gain valuable social currency was irresistible. Neither work nor home, Starbucks provided a place where people could spend their leisure time, socialize, and connect.

The success that Starbucks enjoys is due in no small part to its amazing creation of an organization-specific culture. Customers understand that you can't order a small regular coffee at Starbucks. Instead, you have to ask for a For Here Single Grande White Chocolate Mocha.

Starbucks is about far more than selling coffee. It sells community. Specifically, Starbucks sells exclusive, aspirational community. Starbucks was special because it wasn't for everyone.

While clearly Starbucks hasn't abandoned that initial concept, it has made some choices that seem to be aimed at pursuing what appeared to be low-hanging fruit. There's a chance that this will fundamentally hurt the Starbucks brand over the long term.

When customers were confronted with drive-through windows, a move toward automating in order to serve more customers, and price-driven promotions, they found that they weren't having a unique experience anymore. They were simply buying more expensive coffee in a setting that was eerily reminiscent of the fast-food joints they'd been trying to avoid—and now those fast-food joints have pricey coffee drinks of their own. Starbucks has lost its differentiator.

What makes organizations go off track?

Can Anybody See Me?

What type of person are you least likely to see in a Burger King? Yes, hard-core foodies won't be there, but for a long time, 18- to 35-year-old males, the core demographic of the fast-food industry, weren't there either. Instead, they were at McDonald's. Why?

McDonald's had rapidly adopted the concept of the third place and focused on the experience that its customers got along with their large order of fries. Burger King had chosen to focus on the quality of the product.

There was only one problem with that approach: the largest part of the desired audience didn't actually care all that much about the quality of the burgers they were wolfing down. It's not that Burger King's "have it your way" campaign was bad, per se—it's that it featured a message that the customers had no interest in hearing. The brand became irrelevant. Even now, Burger King is undergoing a convoluted dance to discover that sweet spot where it becomes a default choice for the drive-through diner once again.

What's the best way to recover lost market share from your competition?

You Can't Reach That Bar?

Managing customer expectations has long been considered the Holy Grail of marketing. It's certainly an elusive goal. We'd say it's impossible to achieve if you don't take one critical piece of information into account: customer expectations are not forged by your company; they're created by your competitors.

The customer who is in your store is not judging your merchandise, service, and ambience strictly on their own merits. Your business does not exist in isolation. You do not have the first website your customers have ever seen. Yours is not the first tech support call line they've ever called. You have not hired the first receptionist they've ever met.

In particular industries, the standards have already been established in the minds of many customers. You know the names. Every industry has its own IKEA, its own Harley-Davidson, its own Rolex. These companies have established the baseline for excellence. Every retailer wants its customer service to be considered just as good as Zappos'. Harley-Davidson defines what it means to be a motorcycle. Rolex is synonymous with luxury watches.

These organizations are continually creating the world's view of a category. They are shaping the perceptions, images, and memories that create leading brands. These are the standards your customers have been exposed to. This is what they have in mind when they develop their expectations.

Apple resets the customer expectation bar on an almost daily basis. Stepping into an Apple store is a markedly different experience by design. The Genius Bar, with specially trained employees who will answer any tech question—over and over and over again until you're happy with your ability to use your

Mac, iPhone, or iPad—is a powerful draw. The stores look different. Apple has eliminated cash registers from some of its stores because it doesn't want customers to view shopping at these stores as the typical retail experience.

Customers have responded to this to a degree that exceeded even Apple's own expectations. Stores that were projected to earn $1,000 per square foot earned four times that amount.

Compare that to those businesses that are providing the typical technology retail experience. Witness the demise of Circuit City, or Best Buy's recent decision to slow its expansion plans. These companies are not merely falling behind, they're standing still in the road watching the dust cloud moving farther and farther away. Customers who have experienced what Apple is offering—and note that so far we're talking only about the customer experience, not about the actual products—find the typical experience wanting. Good enough isn't good enough when there's someone else who is continually doing better.

Apple's impact, of course, is on customers, not categories. The customer who has been trained to expect a certain experience when shopping for computers will have those same expectations when shopping for apparel, jewelry, gifts, and electronics and when selecting service providers, medical care, financial guidance, and so on.

The challenge for business owners is great. If you're not providing your customers with a unique and satisfying experience, you are perpetually failing to meet the bar set by an organization that is.

How do you meet that challenge?

Fast, Cheap, Good: Pick Any Two!

Domino's Pizza had built an empire on the promise of fast, cheap, good pizza. However, while it delivered on the fast and cheap portions of the equation, the pizza fell far short of being good.

Customers who had equally priced options available were abandoning the brand in droves until, forced into a position of desperation, Domino's did the unthinkable: it started a campaign that told the public that what it had been doing was terrible, and that it was time for the company to improve its product. It solicited customer feedback, asking for pictures of its pizzas. Then it used those images as part of an ongoing "Mea Culpa" campaign, promising improvement and encouraging customers to be part of its turnaround.

Reinventing the pizza from the crust up may in reality turn out to be nothing more than dumping some new spices into the sauce mix, but it speaks volumes about the lengths to which an organization can be forced to go if it is to recover after it has failed to perform in the way the customer expects.

How do we prevent catastrophic failures in expectation management?

What Else Is Happening?

Every situation we've talked about so far has one thing in common. There is one trait that unites all of them. From Starbucks's awkward foray into the fast lane through Circuit City's shuttered doors and Domino's fundamental failure to provide good pizza, we're looking at scenes that play out in public, in real time on the world stage, visible to all. Anyone who has access to the business pages or is stuck in the airport watching CNN for long enough will hear these stories. They're familiar narratives, even if we don't know what they mean.

But they're not the only problems companies are experiencing. Behind the scenes, off-camera, quiet catastrophes are also playing out in real time, imperiling the very existence of very good companies that are struggling to maintain themselves in one of the toughest economic climates we've ever seen. The fact that these problems aren't as visible, aren't as in-your-face, and aren't as immediately terrifying to management and shareholders doesn't negate their impact.

In fact, when the media do pick up on these problems—something that is increasingly likely, and is happening much faster now that social media are integrated into almost everyone's life—they have just as much potential to break a business.

They're secret trapdoors, embedded in the familiar trail of, "This is how we've always done it." You'll be walking along, with everything appearing to be fine, when suddenly a problem emerges, and you discover that there's empty space directly beneath your feet, where you once took solidity and security completely for granted. Falling puts you and your organization into reactive mode, cleaning up messes and managing spin. This isn't a position any company wants to be in, especially when resources are scarce and crisis management forces them away from revenue producers, such as innovation and production.

Taking On the Trapdoors

GM was once the nation's leading auto manufacturer. It was so successful that it was one of the largest corporations in the nation. It was said that "what's good for the country is good for General Motors, and vice versa." Yet today, it doesn't enjoy quite the same level of prestige, in terms of both productivity and popular acclaim.

GM's slide from dominance was marked by repeated examples of flawed decision making: a focus on automating production that let quality slide substantially, a controversial decision to abandon division branding in favor of an overarching umbrella brand that the public did not either respect or trust, and a never-ending cycle of acquisitions and subsequent divestments of foreign car companies, including Fiat, Suzuki, and Isuzu, brands that its target market did not favor. At the same time, GM discontinued or sold lines that had tremendous customer loyalty, including Oldsmobile, Pontiac, and Saturn.

GM accepted massive amounts of government bailout money as part of the "too big to fail" debacle. It then aired an ad claiming that it had repaid all of the bailout money; this brought a tremendous amount of scorn and governmental censure down upon the company when it was revealed that the money that GM had used to repay the bailout money had actually been borrowed from another government program.

What's missing from this picture?

United Breaks Guitars

To say that the airline industry has had a rough decade is a little like saying that water is wet or that the sun is expected to rise in the east tomorrow. It's a given at this point, with the industry's largest carriers struggling to remain viable, much less competitive.

One might think that given an environment in which costs are escalating, opportunities for profitability are limited, and regulation severely restricts organizational flexibility, a company would perhaps focus on those elements of its business that it has more control over. These areas, such as customer service, provide the best opportunity for an airline to positively differentiate itself without incurring tremendous expense.

Southwest Airlines has done a superb job of this over the years, a fact that Continental, American, and Delta are well aware of. More than a few articles in industry journals have been devoted to analyzing and deconstructing Southwest's success, in the hopes that it is duplicable.

United, however, clearly seemed to have missed the memo. In 2008, musician Dave Carroll witnessed United baggage handlers handling his guitar with less than tender loving care, throwing the expensive instrument onto the tarmac. When Carroll discovered that his $3,500 Taylor guitar was broken, he filed a claim.

Nine months later, still without any compensation from United, Carroll did what musicians do. He wrote a song, performed it with his band, and posted the video on YouTube. It was viewed half a million times in three days, with more than 11 million views to date. This has been a public relations nightmare for United.

Could this have been avoided?

When the Left Hand Doesn't Know Whom the Right Hand Is Selling To

Many organizations suffer from a lack of clarity about the company's customer base, what the people in it value, and why they're loyal. This disconnect can have disastrous consequences, especially when it manifests in ways that make it admirably clear that the company doesn't value its customer base.

Mark Zuckerberg, the founder of Facebook, has been quoted as referring to the social network's first users as "stupid f*cks," which has done little to endear him in the eyes of those who are beginning to view the company less enthusiastically with each new security concern.

In 2009, SCI FI announced that it was changing its name to Syfy, in part to distance the channel from the stereotypical image of the science fiction fan as a nerdy adult, living in his parents' basement and spending his time on World of Warcraft raids. Not only did it turn out that SCI FI's fans were invested in and attached to the stereotypical image and resented the overt goal of changing the association, but the new name was also slang for syphilis in several languages. Fans who felt scorned and disrespected by the rebranding effort wasted no time in sharing that bit of information online.

What can keep a company from self-destruction?

Your First Customers: Attracting and Retaining Good Employees

There is an inverse relationship between economic circumstances and employee retention. The worse the job market is, the easier it becomes to hold onto qualified people. The conviction that there are no other jobs to be found is a powerful incentive to tolerate unpleasant circumstances, substandard pay, and other negative working circumstances. That being said, organizations that thrive based upon the expertise, initiative, and enthusiasm of their employees chronically experience challenges in identifying and retaining great people.

At the same time, socially conscious customers are placing increasing emphasis on how organizations treat their employees. Exxon Mobil, Laclede Group, and Cracker Barrel Old Country Store were all recently listed on the Human Rights Campaign Index as among the worst companies to work for based upon their HR policies. Walmart, undoubtedly the world's largest retailer and one of the most successful businesses ever seen, is regularly savaged by critics who cite its low pay, gender inequalities, and substandard benefits as reasons to stay away. A company can lose considerable amounts of business because of issues that it had previously considered to be wholly internal matters.

How do we conduct business under such scrutiny?

Does It Have to Be like This?

Reading through these examples, one theme keeps coming to the fore: companies get into trouble when they get too far from what their customers want them to be. Not knowing or deviating too far from that set of customer expectations causes organizations to make mistakes at every level in the organization. The wrong choice from the wrong person—whether it's the CEO assessing new locations and brand extension opportunities or the front-line worker faced with an angry customer—can do irreparable damage to a brand. Social networking now gives anyone and everyone a platform upon which to vent her outrage, with the result that brand damage moves faster and is more painful than ever before.

What Are We Missing?

We are suffering from a crucial lack of certainty. Faced with the dynamic and omnipresent challenges that business presents, how do we make good decisions? The only way to avoid the consequences of making bad choices is to make good choices.

How do we do that? We begin with the need for good information, but that's only the starting point. Good information in and of itself is wonderful, but success lies in the interpretation and application of the lessons that are hiding in the data, lessons that often aren't immediately apparent to the casual observer.

We must be able to act with precision and speed, continually positioning our organizations to be receptive and reactive, listening and leading at the same time. Not only do we have to be ahead of the curve, but we have to be able to see the hairpin turn three miles on!

Serious chess fans, even today, revere the performance of Bobby Fischer. During his best days, he was the living embodiment of what great business leaders strive to achieve. Commentators at the time praised Fischer's amazing composure, precise calculation, and devilish resourcefulness, for no matter what scenario an opponent threw at him, with a deftly placed bishop or threatening knight, Fischer knew the countermoves needed to carry the day. Inside his head was a complete library of chess moves and strategies, information that he could access easily and effortlessly at any time to select his next move, steadily and strategically influencing the outcome of the entire game. This information, these data, formed a model that he could use to make the right decision rapidly and repeatedly. So when Fischer lost his queen, as he did in a pivotal game against his renowned rival Tigran Petrosian, he could calmly assess the board, look at what would have been a catastrophic loss for most players, and announce checkmate in two moves.

What we need is a tool that allows businesses to do the same thing.

In the early 1980s, Harley-Davidson was in dire need of such a tool. Japanese companies were destroying the company on pricing. Worse, Harley-Davidson's bikes had lost the quality that made them famous. The brand was dying.

Desperate to save it, Harley executives put themselves at great risk, financing an $80 million buyout. They had only one shot at turning the company around. Every choice they made had to be the right one. There was no room for mistakes. They couldn't afford to idealize their situation or pin their hopes on strategies that would deliver anything less than absolute success.

They needed their own checkmate in two, their own library of moves and strategies that would allow them to be receptive and reactive, and the model that would transform Harley into the dominant force in the motorcycle world once again.

How Do We Identify Opportunity?

The toughest thing to do, but the thing upon which the ultimate success or failure of the company depends, is identifying who your market is. If you don't make the right decision here, you're done. You can have the absolute best product in the world, but if you're trying it to sell it to people who don't want it, you're not going to succeed.

At one time, Snickers was struggling with this very issue, as it was attempting to sell candy bars to people who didn't particularly want candy bars. The company analyzed its sales patterns, hoping to discern who was buying its candy. This research revealed that the peak purchasing times were in mid-afternoon. It turned out that construction workers on break and kids on their way to basketball practice valued the role that Snickers's plentiful peanuts played in quieting rumbling stomachs. This was a pivotal insight. Snickers rebranded itself not as another type of candy, but as a hunger buster. The tagline, "Hungry? Why wait?" helped emphasize the primary value that was already causing people to choose Snickers, an approach that was so effective that today Snickers is the world's leading candy bar.

Nike has a well-established tradition of using high-profile athletes from a range of sports to promote its sneakers. It sells sneakers for 19 different sports, approaching each with the overt "Nike equals victory" message that is nearly impossible for athletes and would-be athletes to resist. This in itself is impressive, and it allows Nike to claim the leadership position in the industry—Adidas, Reebok, and New Balance combined control only 32.6 percent of the market, compared to Nike's 36.3 percent.

More impressive is how Nike used a deep understanding of its target customers to create an entirely new category. When Bo Jackson emerged as a prominent athlete in two sports— football and baseball—Nike partnered with him to promote a line of shoes known as cross trainers. Shoe retailers sell sneakers by sport-specific categories. The addition of an entirely new category for athletes who play more than one sport created an entirely new market. Currently, Nike reports that its athletic trainer line is a $1.4 billion business.

If only there were a tool that gave organizations the ability to do what Snickers and Nike did. There must be a way to tap into and continually meet and exceed customer needs and expectations. If only there were a way to avoid brand-breaking mistakes. If only there were a way to ensure that the decisions being made would ultimately benefit the company and not prove to be embarrassing missteps, talked about later only in hushed tones around the water cooler. If only there were a way to unify every member of an organization, from the newest frontline employee to the CEO, behind a single purpose and way of doing business, creating an appealing, consistent message to customers at every level. If only there were a way to transform customers into stakeholders, giving them an integral role in the business that they would value and reward with ongoing loyalty.

If that existed, it would transform how we do business. It would alter every aspect of our jobs. It would fundamentally rewrite everything we know about being a profitable company and blow open previously untapped opportunities, revealing ways to sell more to our best customers and to transform regular customers into fanatical brand advocates. We would be able to forever alter our strategies, tactics, messages, and performance. That elusive certainty we all long for could be ours, helping to ensure that the decisions we make are good ones, with reasonable expectations of success for each and every campaign.

We could be Disney—or at least the Disney of our industry. We could achieve the position of being not only a category leader but a category definer, transforming the way in which an entire field does business. We could set our own agenda for success, secure in the knowledge that we're creating products that have a market, services that have an audience, and a brand that customers are eager to embrace.

If only we had the tool to make that happen.

The tool exists. It's not a magic silver bullet that will do all the work for you. Using this tool requires you to be on top of your game as a marketer and as a manager. We're talking about leveraging your expertise and know-how with a strategic recognition and integration of the customer's role. We're talking about taking every single person affiliated with your organization, shaking that person by the shoulders, and saying, "There is no business as usual anymore! We must create a new normal!"

If you're ready to do that, if you're ready to experience deep, meaningful organizational change in the name of greater competitiveness, organizational efficiency, and profitability, then hang on. We're about to explore the world of Brand Modeling, and you're never going to be the same again.

CHAPTER 2

Companies Don't Build Brands, Customers Build Brands

What makes a brand a brand? Is it the logo? Is it the language? Can we chalk brand creation up to color choices, product placement, and renting the perfect billboard?

All of those things are important, but none of them builds your brand. What builds a brand is customer attention. If no one knows you're in business, you're not in business. If no one is paying attention to what you're doing, you have no customers. If you have no customers, you have no brand.

That's not what you want to hear—especially if you're the person who is in charge of the time, energy, and resources that your organization puts into building your brand. It's disheartening to learn that your perceived control and ownership of your brand are nothing but an illusion. We all like to think that we're in control of our image. But, a brand is nothing more than a set of collective perceptions—the aggregate of opinions, articulated and analyzed and used as societal shorthand for "those people over there do this to make a living, and this is how they do it."

The customer creates the brand. Customers are the "public" in public perception. Without them, you've got nobody looking at anything. The brands that exist now exist solely because, at some point, for conscious or unconscious reasons, articulated or never given voice, the buying public was engaged in shaping them.

Volkswagens Don't Leak Oil, They Mark Their Spot

In the days after World War II, there were few things that seemed less likely to appeal to the American public than a quirky German car with a hard-to-pronounce name. Yet the Volkswagen Beetle went on to become one of the bestselling cars of all time.

Volkswagen was offering something completely different from what the American auto industry was offering at the time. The distinctively egg-shaped Beetle quickly developed a reputation for reliability and safety, but it was the fact that the idiosyncratic car didn't appeal to everyone that became its strongest selling point.

Customers were drawn to the fact the Beetle was affordable. The economic environment of the 1960s and 1970s, when the little Bug was busily becoming iconic, was not remarkably different from the situation we're in right now. Domestic auto offerings were far more expensive and offered little variety in style or design. Customers loved having an alternative, and they enjoyed owning a car that they felt marked them as both a smart consumer and a free thinker.

Volkswagen returned the love with a distinctive, frank marketing approach, including early print ads that reinforced the exclusive yet ubiquitous appeal of the brand, such as, "Think small," "Some shapes are hard to improve on," and our personal favorite, "Do you earn too much to afford one?" Volkswagen understood that being different was its greatest asset, and it let its customer base define what that difference looked like, what it sounded like, and what it meant. There is no other brand of car with its own children's game—but even today, there are commercials showing even the most distinguished adults playing "punch buggy!"

Even today, Volkswagen is consistently responsive to what its customers value most about the Beetle. It is continually refining both the car and the marketing message to make sure the public knows that it's delivering more individuality, more quirkiness, and more reliable German engineering. The "people's car" appeal of the Beetle's early days in Germany gave way to the rampant individualism of the hippie era, which inspired the eccentric, if pragmatic, aesthetic of today's New Beetle.

Drivers wanted the Beetle. That simple tagline sums up Volkswagen's understanding of branding. It put its customers in the center of the equation, acknowledging their role in defining the brand. This has worked well for the company. Currently, Volkswagen commands 10 percent of the global automotive market—a position it achieved in part because of the success of the Beetle.

Once we understand what Volkswagen knows—once we've reached the point where we can accept as a given the fact that customers are, with varying degrees of conscious acknowledgment of the fact themselves, continually involved in brand building—it's time to start asking the really interesting questions.

Why Do Customers Build Brands?

The obvious first question you have to ask about customers building brands is, why do they bother? Why do customers play any role at all in brand creation? What value comes from the effort? What need are we trying to fulfill when we forge relationships with brands?

When we're talking about needs and what they make us do, we have to talk about humanistic psychologist Abraham Maslow.

Let's start with the understanding that Maslow articulated a hierarchy of needs, each one critical and essential for human life and happiness. On this hierarchy, Maslow put the need to belong to groups just after the needs for health and safety. The need to belong is absolutely fundamental to our existence.

As a species, we come hardwired with the need to join. On a very deep level, we want to be part of the group. We want to be surrounded by people we feel bonded to. If you look at this from an evolutionary perspective, you can talk about how primitive humans formed tribes to make survival easier, dividing labor, sharing resources, and developing complex systems to ensure that everyone received some measure of care, even when he was most vulnerable. This is how society was born. We live better lives when we form groups. Shift to a retail perspective: it's fun to go on a shopping spree, but it can be more fun shopping with your friends. It doesn't matter if the underlying motivation is deadly serious or seriously trivial. We are driven to belong. That need is part of what defines us.

For a long time, we fed this need with our social institutions. We could define ourselves geographically: we were where we came from. This was refined into all the nuances of class and community, delineating to the nth degree who we were by our connections: Where did we go to school? To work? To church? This is still true to some degree. It means something to be a Harvard alum, a Teamster, or a Southern Baptist.

Some of our societal structures simply aren't as strong as they used to be, however. Anything created by humans is subject to human frailties, and we see this weakness take its toll on organizations of every size, from the smallest school board to the largest church in the world. Seeing once-treasured institutions stumble, or even fail, is a distressing phenomenon for some people. No one likes being distressed, and so people protect their psyches and reduce their emotional investments with the group. They stop going to meetings, they stop identifying themselves as part of the group, and they stop considering the organization as a factor in their decision-making process.

When individualism is held in high regard, as it is in the United States, the appeal of these institutional societal structures is weakened further. If there's no penalty—no public censure, no criticism, and no impact personally or professionally—for not belonging to a group, and there's no overwhelming perceived benefit to be gained by participation, most people will happily opt out.

This is especially true when there are intangible social benefits from going your own way. Whether it's the eccentric, the entrepreneur, or the exceptional, our society celebrates and recognizes most those people who have forged their own way in the world, defining themselves and their excellence (or lack thereof) by how they differ from the rest of society, not by how well they mesh into it.

Factor in a culture in which leisure time is at a premium, yet participation in traditional societal structures demands hours on a regular basis, and we find that congregations grow smaller, town meetings go unattended, and the work of creating community goes undone.

When that happens, a very real aspect of community is lost. It's not at all unusual for people not to know their next-door neighbors, much less who lives two streets over in that new blue house. You might get a nod of recognition in the grocery store parking lot if you're lucky, but actually knowing about the people who surround you? It's an increasingly rare phenomenon.

The community may be gone, but the hunger for it is not. Maslow has told us that the need to belong will not be denied. We need to belong more than we need to establish our own unique identity. Our affiliations are a compulsory element of our selves. If we can't supply that element effectively using the traditional social structures, we'll find something else that will work. It's essential that we have those relationships, and in a fascinating cultural evolution, we've used the fields of commerce to hunt for meaning.

This meaning can be esoteric and profound, or it can be something as simple (and as life-changing) as choosing to look at the sunnier side of life. That's the approach that one small T-shirt company used to transform itself into a million-dollar brand.

When It's Done Right: Life Is Good

For five years, Bert and John Jacobs sold T-shirts on the streets of Boston, and door-to-door in college dorms all over the East Coast. They didn't have a storefront, but they did have a van, which doubled as a warehouse, an office, and their sleeping quarters on most nights. Taking that van coast to coast helped them sell a few more shirts than they were able to hawk on foot, but business was hardly booming.

Then the brothers decided that a doodle hanging on their apartment wall, a character that they christened Jake, belonged on a T-shirt. Jake has a big, contagious smile—there's nothing of the brooding artist type about him. He was faithfully paired with the same words, "Life is good."

The character and the message instantly resonated with customers. They sold out of their first run of 48 shirts at a street fair.

It didn't take long for Bert and John to recognize that Jake's appeal lay in his optimistic attitude. Jake could do anything. Soon he was appearing (joined by his trust dog Rocket) on Frisbees, backpacks, coffee mugs, and T-shirts in every color of the rainbow.

Today, The Life is good Company has a presence that stretches from coast to coast. This T-shirt company differentiated itself from millions of other apparel vendors by listening to what its best customers really wanted—a message of optimism and happiness in a far-too-prone-to-be-bleak world—and delivered it. More important even than the message is the sense of community that surrounds the brand. The T-shirts serve as a sort of visual shorthand. Life is good fans can express their optimistic outlook, identify others who feel the same way about the world, and celebrate that new connection.

The T-shirts are only the starting point. There are Life is good festivals, attended by legions who appreciate the humor, simple wisdom, and sense of fun associated with the brand. Fans flock to the company's Facebook page for doses of uplifting inspiration and to share their own thoughts on what makes life good. They're participating in a community of optimism. Appealing to these hardwired needs, especially the need to belong, has enabled Life is good to reach an enviable place in a competitive market.

What Do Brands Do for Their Customers?

The power and prominence of brands, particularly those powerful Cult Brands with a devoted following, are proof positive that society is ready to bond with companies the way it once bonded with communities, schools, and churches.

Strong brands make this easy by offering their customers a number of benefits. There are tangible benefits—the product or service—and, far more important, the intangible qualities that form a critical part of the brand's appeal.

Customers Build Brands by Building Themselves

Every one of us has a life to build, an identity to create, and a self to realize and then, eventually, come to peace with. There are countless ways to do this, but we're just going to focus on how we, as consumers, define ourselves through our purchasing decisions.

In many ways, we are what we buy. Let's look at the "executive uniform" of suit and tie that we wear to the office. It may be that as we advance through our career and want to make more of an impression, suddenly only an Hermès tie will do. We have to have a Bulgari watch, not because it tells time with any more accuracy than any other kind of timepiece, but because we're the type of person who would wear Bulgari to the office. We need our accessories to be in alignment with our self-image.

Harley-Davidson understands and leverages the power of branding as a tool of self-definition better than any other organization on the planet. It sponsors the Harley Owners Group for its customers and isn't the least bit shy about articulating that HOG membership is about far more than joining a bike club. "It's one million people around the world united by a common passion: making the Harley-Davidson dream a way of life," it says on the group's website, explicitly joining an aspirational lifestyle with the Harley brand.

Whether or not people hear those exact words, they clearly get the message. If you want to be a biker, if you want your share in the chrome-pipe dream of open roads, good times, and freedom, you need a Harley. We're talking about more than a bike; we're talking about building your life around a dream held in common with others.

This applies in every industry, every sector, and every category. We see it in finance: the E*TRADE investor who prides himself on going it alone is a fundamentally different customer from the Charles Schwab customer who wants the comfort of being able to "talk to Chuck." The woman who buys a Coach bag is a fundamentally different woman from the one who gets a hiking pack at REI and figures it'll serve double duty on the rare occasions when she needs a purse. We make purchases that reinforce our self-image—or at least as close as our budget allows us to get to our self-image. All things being equal, customers will always opt to go for the brand that does the most for them.

It's the ultimate in self-determinism, in a way. If you want that Harley lifestyle, and you have several thousand spare dollars, you can buy your way into it. The actual motorcycle is only a small fraction of the Harley brand. Consider the apparel, the merchandise, and the hundreds of thousands of shield-shaped tattoos. All of these give a person a way to signal his desire to belong to the Harley community. Harley teaches us all a valuable lesson when it demonstrates that the most desirable aspect of any prospect is his enthusiasm for the group. Secondary by far is his immediate ability to buy the product.

Who Am I to You? Who Am I to Me?

A brand can offer personal validation. In addition to helping us define ourselves to others, our relationship with brands can help us become more comfortable with or confident in the identities that we choose for ourselves.

Connecting with a company, buying its products, participating in its forums, forging connections online, and being able to refer the company to friends gives the customer a chance to view herself in a positive light by association. I may be a smart businessperson, but I'm smarter when I stay at Holiday Inn Express. Choosing one hotel over another doesn't create intelligence, of course, but that's not what marketing is about. Instead, we're talking about giving customers a way to highlight and reinforce those aspects of their own personalities that they value.

Buying a Mac doesn't make someone more creative, intelligent, inventive, or endearingly eccentric, but Apple aficionados proudly claim all of those labels for themselves. The iEmpire thrives by providing products with aesthetics, functionality, and brand personality that are in alignment with its market's core values.

This validation can come delivered as a story, a type of personal narrative that the customer can and wants to identify with. Just by lighting a cigarette, a man can feel more rugged, tough, independent, and brave—as long as the cigarette is a Marlboro.

Some stories are a little broader and more universal in nature. Brands often attempt to align themselves to fit one of these universal stories. If they try to reach the audience for the "Good Mom" story, it's a safe bet that this audience will be large enough. The hunger and drive to be a good mom are so strong and so universal that this story can be used to connect with customers on a number of levels. We see choosy moms choosing Jif, Disney offering iPhone apps to help moms ensure that their families get maximum enjoyment out of the Magic Kingdom, and Nintendo Wii enjoying unprecedented increases in market penetration as the game console is presented as a way to bring families together.

Where Do I Fit in This Great Big World?

A sense of community is one of the most powerful benefits a brand can offer. Volkswagen owners know this well, with the fluid edges of the Bug-loving world being defined by the enthusiastic legions of punch-buggy players, who pummel their acquaintances' arms whenever one of the distinctive vehicles drives by. Exclusivity and being "in the know" have their own heady cachet. Savvy brands are very aware of how they control access to information, and they make a point of ensuring that their devoted fans are among the first to know.

We see this play out often in the film industry, where the buzz can make or break a picture within a week of the film's release. Engagement with the fan community was so pivotal to the team making Peter Jackson's *Lord of the Rings* films that when ardent fans tried to sneak onto the set and get inside information before the film's completion, they were first formally escorted off of the set and then invited back for a proper tour, forming the beginning of a unique two-directional conversation between a creative team and its intended audience that played a pivotal role in the film's blockbuster success. Even now, years after the films have all been released, the community remains active—boding well for future films from both Jackson and the *Lord of the Rings* franchise.

What About My Needs? What Does the Customer Do for the Brand?

It's all been pretty altruistic so far, hasn't it? All this understanding and insight and what the brand does for the customer. What about what the customer does for the brand?

For the vast majority of customers, the answer to that is going to be "not much." But a small percentage—a percentage that is growing steadily with the prominence of social media—will make a conscious decision to form a relationship with your brand. From those who are generally favorable toward you to tattooed-with-your-logo brand fanatics, this percentage of customers will constitute the lion's share of your business.

The more enamored a customer is of your brand, the more he'll do for you. Making recommendations and creating referral business, participating in events hosted by or involving your organization, joining online discussion groups, or liking the company's Facebook page—truly ardent customers seek out as many ways as possible to connect. They place a high premium on information about the businesses they admire.

There's even a type of meta-observation going on now, where organizations are being judged based upon their responsiveness to customer groups—those organizations that seem to be the most responsive and aware are viewed more positively and as being worthy of customer dollars.

The elephant in the center of the room, of course, is customer information. Almost as valuable as direct sales is the absolute wealth of information and data that customers are willing to volunteer in the name of forging a stronger relationship with a brand. If it is harnessed appropriately, this information helps your overall organizational performance improve tremendously.

You can streamline your decision-making processes, avoid marketing missteps, and enjoy a greater return on every investment you make in your business if you know how to get maximum value out of what your best customers will happily tell you.

With Great Power Comes Great Responsibility

A highly valued brand relationship does not grant your company any sort of free pass. It's not a silver bullet that you can use to vanquish internal problems, less-than-stellar customer service, or the fact that your website looks like it was designed as a sixth grader's extra credit project. Quite the opposite. It could be argued that it is the customers who are most devoted to and passionate about a brand that are its fiercest critics.

Apple knows this lesson well, having learned it more than a few times. Its fanatical customer base will shell out top dollar and endure waiting lists and allocation lotteries when there's just not enough product to go around, but when issues of content censorship in the iApp store and an iPad that failed to deliver the functionality that its purported target market would value the most arise, the criticisms come fast, furious, and with pinpoint precision to the platforms where they'll be seen by the maximum number of people in the minimum amount of time.

The message is clear: if you want the relationship with us, if you value our support and enthusiasm and the fact that we'll circle the block at four in the morning to be the first in the door for the latest iGadget, you've got to know that we're going to be right there critiquing your performance and analyzing every aspect of how you do what you do. If you want our love, the customers say, you'd better be continually proving yourself worthy of it.

Timid companies may back away at this point, unsure whether they can survive the pressure of this much scrutiny.

Isn't there a way to reap the reward, they wonder, without taking so much risk?

We have a really long answer for this question, but let us sum it up first for you by saying no. You can't risk-manage your way into greatness. That's like trying to unicycle your way into respectability, all the while wearing giant sunglasses, a rainbow wig, and a big red clown nose.

You can't avoid risk entirely, no matter what you do, and we'd argue that playing it safe by aping the actions of larger, more successful companies without being willing to take the great big scary chances that they're willing to take is actually a greater risk to your organization's future. You're limiting your routes to opportunity.

For example, there's not a hotelier out there that doesn't know the Ritz-Carlton name. For generations, Ritz-Carlton has been the gold standard. Its employees pride themselves on being "ladies and gentlemen serving ladies and gentlemen." That doesn't sound particularly risky until you see this concept in action.

Consider the server who, after being faced with an increasingly belligerent and inappropriate customer in the dining room, showed him the door. When this action was questioned by a consultant, who was aghast at the thought of a mere server turning away business, the server replied that the customer was not a gentleman. Obviously, the customer did not belong at the Ritz.

Every employee at the Ritz-Carlton is empowered to spend up to $2,000 to make the customer happy. If that means comping a room, then the room is comped. You could be *any* employee of the Ritz and have this authority: the groundskeeper, the housekeeping staff, absolutely anyone.

The Ritz believes this is part of the formula for providing the ultimate in service, the part of its brand that is most highly valued by its customers. It's not a secret. This isn't proprietary knowledge. Yet you can go to dozens of other major hotels and find that the staff members are not similarly empowered. The decision has been made that the potential risk—apparently of staff members handing out rooms for the most capricious of reasons—far outweighs the benefits of amazing its customers.

The Ritz took the risk. That's why everybody knows its name.

Customers Are Already Leading. Are You Ready to Follow?

A relationship is good only if it's good for both parties. It takes time, insight, good data, and some pretty hard-core analysis to identify that perfect spot where customer enthusiasm and organizational profitability are at the maximum levels, and until that point is reached, you need to be sure that you're maintaining observable momentum in the right direction or risk losing the customer base you have, never mind not attracting more traffic.

In the coming chapters, we'll be looking intensely at what's involved in achieving what Apple, Volkswagen, and Harley have done. For now, it's important that you stop and recognize that what we're talking about is a fundamentally different way of doing business than what you've previously been accustomed to. Opening up your decision-making process to make it more responsive to what your best customers value most about your organization, in order to refine and enhance it even further, can be a scary prospect. We promise you, right here, right now, that that fear lasts only as long as it takes for the success to start. Confidence is built one triumph at a time. Then you get very comfortable about hearing from your customers because you know it makes your business better.

Listening to your customers means more than using social media as marketing tools. You wouldn't know this from browsing the business section at the local bookstore or flipping through a marketing magazine, but it's true. There's so much focus on getting famous on Facebook or becoming the talk on Twitter (for all of a day, a day and a half being longer than eternity itself online) that we've lost sight of what social media really are, what are simply tools to facilitate conversation.

What social media have done, in a nutshell, is create an atmosphere in which customer expectations have been allowed to blossom unchecked. Customers know what they want, they know how to make themselves heard, and they know that they can easily, effectively, and efficiently leverage the force of a million like-minded individuals to attempt to force organizations to act in the way they deem best. Consumers are refining entitlement into an art form. Many expect better than real-time responsiveness from the companies they deal with. Heaven help the company with a customer complaint that has to wait until "the next business day"—the world doesn't accommodate that pace anymore.

Believe it or not, this is a good thing—a really good thing. What we have here is the terrible beauty of a culture that is becoming self-aware. Customers are starting to really understand the power they have over the organizations they do business with and, along with that sense of entitlement, riding in the cooler shadow of fury and outrage and Bring Back the Obscure Product No One Ever Bought Until We Stopped Selling It petitions, is something even fantastic. It's emotional engagement. It's investment. It's a feeling of ownership. This is the sentiment that leads customers to defend companies online and in person; the emotion that drives people to attend meet-ins and road trips across state lines; the passion that transforms brands into icons.

This is the raw material that we use to build Brand Models. These are the models we use to build companies beyond all expectation until they occupy that ideal spot, that Promised Land, where there is no competition, only emulation and imitation.

Where It Counts the Most

- Dominant organizations aren't for everyone. Winning companies know who their best customers are and what they want. Nothing else matters!
- Dominant organizations aren't defined by their products or services. They're defined by the critical differences that their best customers value most.
- Cultural changes have resulted in people turning to commercial enterprises (brands) for needs that were formerly met by other types of organizations. We may not go to church anymore, but we feel community with others who drive the same car, wear the same clothes, and participate in the same activities.
- We search for experiences that meet our needs. When a brand does a good job of meeting our psychological needs, we keep doing business with it, even to the point of choosing that brand above all others. Dominant organizations are those with brands that do the best job of meeting their customers' psychological needs.
- Dominant organizations make it easier for their customers to be the people they want to be. They provide positive reinforcement, connecting purchasing decisions with specific values that resonate deeply with their customer base.
- Stories and cultural narratives play a critical role in how our customers see themselves and the world around them. If you know the story that your customers value most, you'll be able to reach them more effectively than your competitors will.
- Customers value a sense of community, of being connected to other people who share the same values and enthusiasms that they themselves have.

- Love is its own reward. Customers who love your brand will take active steps that will help your organization become even more successful. These steps will include doing lots of business with your company, referring your company to family and friends, and, most important of all, participating in the community that surrounds your organization.
- Dominant organizations know that customers are seeking ways to connect with the companies they admire. They provide frequent opportunities for customer connection, and they are highly responsive to customer input.
- Fortune favors the bold. Dominant organizations take on the risks inherent in being great. They're willing to take chances, ignore how "everyone else does it," and commit themselves to providing what their best customers value most about the brand.

PART II

Modeling Defined

CHAPTER 3

What Is Modeling?

It was the last week of June 2010. In the Gulf of Mexico, BP was struggling to stop the world's largest oil spill. Some initial progress had been made when bad news hit: the first storm of the season, eventually known as Hurricane Alex, was beginning to form.

Would this add another layer of trouble to BP's plate of catastrophe? Hurricane conditions would force evacuation, meaning that the oil containment and recovery efforts would stop. Countless gallons of oil would spew unchecked.

Yet failing to evacuate if the storm approached wasn't an option. The potential loss of life was too great, and for a company that was already under fire for irresponsibility, even the appearance of being capricious with its workers' safety wasn't acceptable.

Would BP stay or would it go? More important to our discussion here, how would BP's leadership make the decision?

The most important criteria to consider at this point were the strength and direction of the storm. How close was Alex going to get to the spill? How strong was it going to be when it got there? It would be impossible to make a rational decision to stay or to go without accurate answers to these questions.

Getting those answers is easier said than done. Hurricanes don't file flight plans. There's no way to tell from simple observation which way the storm's going to blow. Satellite pictures can tell you moment by moment where the storm is, but they do not show you where the storm is going.

For that, you need a model. A model uses the available, pertinent data to predict future events. In the case of our Hurricane Alex example, we'd be looking for information on previous hurricanes and everything that influenced their behavior, such as water temperature and wind currents, then analyze that information, looking for statistical correlations. Looking at the behavior of storms that formed in the same way and exhibited the same characteristics that the nascent storm Alex was now exhibiting provided a framework upon which it was possible to predict, with a relatively high degree of accuracy and confidence, the path of the hurricane.

The value of a model becomes clear once you start asking, "What if?" What if Hurricane Alex crossed a body of warm water? Would it speed up, slow down, or change direction? What if a strong west wind kicked up? Could it force the storm back to sea, slow it down, or move it dangerously near the oil spill site? Every outcome could be considered, with objective analysis pinpointing the most likely scenarios.

This predictive model was critical to the BP leadership. It showed Hurricane Alex coming ashore safely to the southwest of BP's position. The company could continue its operations confident that staying in place and continuing cleanup and containment efforts was the better decision. Also avoided was the very high environmental and PR cost for being overly cautious and shutting down operations unnecessarily.

Cooking Up Success: Modeling in the Kitchen

We're not all running deep-sea oil drilling operations. One thing we are all doing, however, is eating, and eating means cooking, which brings us to a great demonstration of modeling at work: the recipe.

Iron Chefs are made, not born. There's no such thing as a natural cook, who intuitively knows how to take a chicken and magically produce down-home fried drumsticks or banh tam cari, depending on the diner's pleasure. Everyone who knows how to cook a dish at some point had to learn how to cook it.

What happens when you want to cook something you've never made before? You don't have to start the process entirely from scratch. Let's say you want some cheesecake. What's the first step? Get a good recipe.

A recipe is, essentially, a predictive model. With its ingredient list and carefully numbered steps, your cheesecake recipe draws on the best-known relevant data about cheesecake making. The recipe guides you through the process, eliminating any uncertainty and increasing the chances that you'll enjoy the cake once it's finished.

There are literally hundreds of different cheesecake recipes, each slightly different from the next. This reflects the fact that you're trying to reach a subjective standard—the "best" cheesecake is different for each of us. Some folks like classic creamy perfection, with nothing but the flavor of the cheese itself to delight the palate, while others prefer cheesecakes that contain chocolate, nuts, or other goodies. Neither school is right or wrong, but if you want to achieve a certain type of cheesecake, you're going to need to use the right recipe. The quality of the end result is dependent upon the model used to create it.

An effective model must recognize and include all of the parameters necessary for success. The ingredient list must be complete. You can't leave anything out, or the results will be different from what you'd anticipated. A cheesecake made without the needed sugar isn't going to win rave reviews.

If you follow the model, however, you eliminate a great deal of uncertainty. You also save a lot of time. No effort or energy is wasted trying to figure out the best way to achieve the desired outcome. You can chart your course based upon what's worked before.

That's where the cheesecake recipe helps us out. You don't have to guess about what type of cheese to use, how much sugar you need, or how hot the oven needs to be. The recipe gives you a free pass out of the trial-and-error cooking school. The recipe contains all of that information based directly on the recipe author's previous cheesecake experience. What worked for him, the logic goes, will work for you. All you have to do is follow the model.

Uncertainty is eliminated. You have a reasonable chance of a dependable outcome. You can rest assured that what you're getting for your efforts is a cheesecake. You're not going to open up the oven and find pumpkin pie in there.

That is, of course, if you adhere to the recipe. If you follow the model, you will get the projected result. It works in the kitchen, and it works in business. That's why so much attention is paid to successful companies. It's smart and strategic to identify and emulate what they're doing right, so that we can have the same success in our own companies.

The more you cook, the more it becomes clear that a recipe is a framework designed to create a given dish. Once you've mastered a recipe—that is, once you've gained a complete and thorough understanding of what the model is and how it operates—you can begin to adapt it.

These adaptations might arise out of necessity. If you don't have quite enough ingredients for the traditional-size cheesecake, can you adapt the recipe for a smaller portion?

These adaptations might also arise out of inventiveness. The recipe allows us to predict, with a reasonable degree of accuracy, what will happen if we change things around. What if we substitute cherries for blueberries, cocoa for chocolate, or orange liqueur for orange juice?

Experienced cooks soon learn that you can fine-tune and tweak a recipe almost infinitely as long as you don't mess with the fundamental concepts that make the dish "work." Cheesecake batter can be neither too liquid nor too dry, which means that any recipe, any model, must contain the right balance of liquid and dry ingredients. The strength of a model is in identifying these core elements, their relationship with each other, and the impact of making changes. The better the model, the more accurately it will predict outcomes.

Setting Stars in Heaven: Modeling in Space

It was July 1969. The *Apollo 11* mission was a success, putting mankind on the moon and conquering one of the great unknowns.

This was cutting-edge modeling in action. Scientists were attempting to run a mission based upon pure prediction. Remember that no one knew with absolute certainty that you could land a spacecraft upon the moon. No one knew with absolute certainty that the moon's gravity would be sufficient to keep the astronauts on it. No one could say definitively that the spacecraft could launch itself once again from the lunar surface and return home, splashing down safely, or that the men inside would survive the trip. Those designing the mission were confronted with the rarest of challenges: a complete lack of precedent.

It's easy to forget, especially given the way in which scientific news is presented by the media, how little we actually know about space. We can't say with confidence where anything actually is at any given point in time—planets, asteroids, or comets. We use models to predict where those objects are, but we don't know if we're accurate. It's not as if we can drive to

Pluto and check. In some cases, it's hard to even catch a glimpse of what's happening, much less analyze whether the scenario is playing out the way the scientists projected that it should.

You begin to see some of the challenges of space exploration. Lacking any firsthand data about the lunar environment, scientists had to construct a model based upon what they knew. Research conducted in the planet's most extreme conditions, high in the atmosphere where the oxygen is thin and gravity little more than a memory, had to provide a framework strong enough and accurate enough to send men, a machine, and a nation's hope out into space.

There could be no higher stakes.

The success of the *Apollo 11* mission and our subsequent history of space exploration have validated those early models. Based only on what was known and verifiable, people constructed the theoretical models necessary to navigate a wholly unknown environment.

Another important function of models became clear throughout the life of the space program. Beginning with those earliest rockets, valuable data were gathered during each mission that could be analyzed and then integrated into what had previously been known about space travel. Further missions would be better prepared for space, initiating a cycle of perpetual improvement as those missions returned with even more relevant data to affect further exploration. This cycle represents the only environment in which growth and innovation can occur, a setting rich with highly accurate, relevant, and timely information.

The model evolved as it was used, becoming richer and more valuable, and incorporating an entire body of knowledge and institutional effort toward one common goal. Everything was focused on the safe exploration of space. Adherence to a model can create a unity of purpose, a single-minded vision that's absolutely essential to success.

There will always be uncertainty. There is no point where we will know everything there is to know about space travel. We're never going to understand every aspect of customer behavior. However, we can, through effective use of models, manage uncertainty to such a degree that we can act confidently, decisively, and well.

Way More than Weather: Model Use in the Wild

Scientists, economists, and researchers of every type create and use models on a regular basis. Modeling is critical in any endeavor where we're trying to make the best possible decision in a situation in which many variables are not only unknown but unknowable. The greater the number of unknown variables in the situation, the greater the need for a model to project what could potentially happen. You want to answer the question, "What if?" as completely as possible.

Every time the Federal Reserve adjusts interest rates, it makes the decision based upon extensive research and economic modeling. How did the market respond the last time the Fed raised rates a point, or let them drop half a point? Keeping rates steady can have a very positive effect on the economy, or it can be seen as a portent of dark economic times ahead, shaking consumer confidence. The impact of the decisions that the Fed makes is so great that it must model reactions and responses ahead of time.

"What if?" is a critical question, but it's not the only question. Modeling provides us with a wide range of highly relevant, accurate information that we need if we are to make the best business decisions consistently.

Like a recipe, a model guides us to success. Identifying and articulating what the fundamental aspects of an organization's success are provides the operational parameters so critical to effective leadership. We need to know what the constants are—the unique factors that define us favorably in our customers' minds. Understanding the key attributes of your best customers and your brand itself simplifies every aspect of corporate communications, crystallizing what your marketing must do, and why. This provides an element of organizational stability, removing uncertainty in a dynamic environment of changing trends and mobile markets.

A model plays a crucial role in defining the processes that are essential for success. By clearly articulating the desired goal, the model simplifies the decision-making process. NASA makes decisions based on a single criterion: will this help our spacecraft and people get safely into space? If the answer is no, the idea's a nonstarter. This saves time, energy, and resources at every level of the organization, from the decision makers to those who have to implement the decisions.

Staples doesn't sell crystal balls. You can check Office Depot, Viking, and Office Max, and there's still nothing. Walk every aisle; scrutinize every website; spend as much time as you need to convince yourself that in the marketplace today, there's no tool that allows business owners to see into the future.

That's part of the reason why leading business scholars and researchers, including Henry Chesbrough and Richard Rosenbloom of Harvard Business School, have been advocating for the embrace of modeling by the business world. The predictive abilities inherent in the concept of modeling that can track hurricanes and launch rockets can be used to analyze customer behavior and provide valuable insight, enabling better decision making.

We take the concept a little further. Strategic use of modeling applied to an individual brand can provide a competitive advantage that is unbeatable in today's marketplace. In the next chapter, we'll be discussing how Brand Modeling, or the synthesis of enhanced customer insight, organizational efficiency, and a complete unity of vision, gives companies the ability to occupy the dominant position in their markets, the place where competition becomes irrelevant.

Modeling Means Measurement

The immediate and obvious implication of knowing what your customers value the most about your brand is as a way to improve performance and identify opportunities.

Once the constants have been identified, they can be measured. This set of measurements can be used to set benchmarks, highlighting your strengths and pinpointing where you're not actually connecting with your best customers all that well.

Harley-Davidson is now the strongest motorcycle brand in the world, but that wasn't always the case. The 1970s were a disastrous period for the company. The quality and reliability of Harley-Davidsons had slipped so badly that the company was in danger of going under. A desperate buyout bid would pay off only if the new leadership could bring bikers back to Harley and attract a new generation of customers.

To do that, Harley-Davidson needed to know, quickly and accurately, what would bring customers back. This required more than identifying and rectifying problems. "It's not terrible anymore!" is not a strong selling proposition. Instead, Harley-Davidson delved deeply into what qualities the brand's best customers—the most loyal of the loyal—valued most about the Harley brand. Measuring and quantifying the intangible characteristics that made Harley attractive to its best customers provided part of the framework necessary to improve performance.

The camaraderie and sense of freedom-loving brotherhood that Harley lovers held in high regard became the framework of the Harley Owners Group. It was possible to capitalize on this branding proposition only after Harley's leaders became aware of the size and magnitude of the underlying needs that motivated people to buy Harleys. Having data on those needs gave Harley-Davidson a route to action that strengthened its bond with its best customers, and this subsequently strengthened its position in the marketplace.

Harley-Davidson executed a dramatic turnaround. You may not be facing such dire straits in your organization. That doesn't mean you're exempt from problems, existing or emerging. Maybe your best customers love your merchandise, but dislike having to deal with your customer service department if there's a problem. An effective model will do more than identify these trouble spots. It will help you assess the most strategic, effective way to transform your weaknesses into strengths. If addressing those issues would increase your organization's portion of the customer's wallet—through an additional sale or larger sales—you'll see this play out in the model. Making changes in actual performance to reach idealized benchmarks will have a positive impact on your organization's financial health.

Change for Change's Sake? Not Anymore

Brand Modeling, as we've conceived it, shines as a predictive tool. It was designed to answer one of the most challenging questions any business leader faces—the dreaded "What if?" Nothing in business is fixed, and we need to be able to predict with a reasonable degree of accuracy what would happen if we changed one of the factors that is currently recognized as a constant. When you have a Brand Model, you have a concrete understanding of all the critical patterns inherent in your brand that position it uniquely in the customer's mind. In other words, you know what makes you *you*, and, more important, you know why your customers choose you more often than they choose the competition.

For example, the theme park industry knows at least some of its critical patterns. A theme park's success depends upon its ability to wow its audience. It has to deliver a thrilling experience every time, to every customer. Disney has near-perfect knowledge of these patterns. There are fundamental differences between the Disney theme park experience and any other theme park experience that extend far beyond considerations of scale. Brand Modeling examines the consumer trends, market changes, and other variables that lead the eager fun seeker to choose one park over another.

Brand Modeling can help park owners decide what changes would attract more business their way and encourage the customers they've already captured to do more business with them. They will learn what it will take to persuade families to take a second trip to the park in a year, or a third trip—or to have their family reunion or wedding within the theme park.

Increasing the wow factor is a no-brainer, but what changes will offer the most reward? Using a Brand Model to measure what would happen if a theme park owner could increase the wow factor by 5 percent provides the framework necessary to make smart, strategic decisions. If raising the wow factor means building a new attraction, will the projected rise in attendance cover the cost? Is it smarter to build two smaller rides and raise the wow factor by 7 percent, incurring greater expense initially, but with a greater projected attendance rate? Are there ways to increase the wow factor that aren't as cost-intensive as building new attractions, yet will still be valued highly by the most loyal customers?

Models are designed to be multifaceted, taking into account numerous aspects of customer behavior—not only those that the customers can articulate for themselves.

What Bar Are You Trying to Reach?

In-depth customer insight is required to inform a comprehensive Brand Model. When our base has told us what it values about our brands, and we delve deeply into the underlying psychological traits that facilitate that alignment, we wind up with a series of benchmarks and criteria that constitute the heart of a brand.

What's in Disney's heart? It's all about the magic. Disneyland is the place where dreams come true. There's the Magic Kingdom and the Disney Magic cruise line. Every decision that Disney makes, from the largest expansion plans to the smallest detail of employee training, has to meet one test first: does this contribute to the magic of Disney?

In other words, are you on brand or off brand? This is a question that you can't answer without a rock-solid understanding of what your brand is in your customer's eyes. Your Brand Model serves as the framework for evaluating possible outcomes, ensuring that you continually meet and exceed your own standards. More important, you'll be meeting and exceeding your customer's expectations, a sure route to organizational success.

The stronger and more integrated the Brand Model, the more successful the organization can become. It's hard to think of a more definitive example of a successful integrated Brand Model than that of Nike, a company that has achieved the enviable position of being able to shape its customers as much as its customers shape it.

Nike's understanding of its customer base has given it an enviable level of predictability. Having sold many billions of dollars worth of athletic shoes, the company knows that it doesn't have to reinvent the wheel. It must simply make sure that the rims are painted the exact color that the customer can't live without! In this instance, that means having the right celebrity endorsement—from a dominant, perhaps iconic, athlete—coupled with the perfect pithy, aggressively optimistic catchphrase, the de facto passwords into the country of cool. It's more than a formula that works. It is a model that can flex and adapt to continually meet changing customer demands while consistently delivering what customers value most.

Again, we come back to the "What if?" question. A Brand Model allows us to ask, "What if we do this? Will it make our brand stronger?" and gives us objective, statistical information that allows us to answer these questions.

A Better Model Means a Better Business

The Wiz is gone. Crazy Eddie has gone, almost silently, into the night. Computer City failed, followed later by Circuit City. RadioShack is hanging on to the last frayed length of speaker wire with both hands, about to fall forever into the abyss of irrelevancy, but Best Buy stands strong, the nation's largest consumer electronics retailer. It currently controls nearly 20 percent of the domestic market, and it is becoming increasingly influential overseas.

Why does Best Buy remain when other companies have folded? What is it doing differently?

Every one of the chains mentioned sold the same type of merchandise as Best Buy does. But only Best Buy pushed past the concept that it was "just selling electronics" and delved deeply into why people were buying from it.

During this phase, Best Buy discovered that it had four primary types of customers. It identified why given groups of people choose to shop at Best Buy, and structured its stores to appeal to whichever of the four types of customers was most predominant in a particular area. The creation of the Geek Squad, a friendly, nonthreatening band of experts who actually know how to install and service computer systems, smoothly met a largely unarticulated need, alleviating a customer's fear that she would not be able to hook up all of the technology she had just purchased, much less actually use it.

Anyone can sell you a television. Best Buy's attention to its customers taught it how to sell the experience of buying a television without worry. Its approach to modeling taught it a critical point of differentiation, one that Best Buy has leveraged so effectively that it's the most dominant player in the category today.

So now we're clear on what modeling can do in general. Now it's time to delve into what modeling means for business—and for your brand.

Where It Counts the Most

- There will be times when you need to make strategic and smart decisions in the absence of complete information. Modeling provides leaders with a predictive tool that guides decision making in even the most uncertain environments.

- Modeling provides credible, actionable answers to the question, "What if?" The comprehensive nature of Brand Modeling considers every variable that affects decision making. Leaders can see the impact of decisions before they act on them.

- Brand Models reveal opportunities for change and growth while articulating the inalienable parameters of customer expectation.

- Brand Models are dynamic instruments. They can evolve as market experience and real-world data become available to replace the theoretical. Each refinement of the model makes it—and the business decisions you make using it—better.

- Identifying the constants—those key elements of your brand that your best customers value most—simplifies the decision-making process. Choices can be weighed against a single criterion: do they move an organization closer to its goals or further away from them?

- Brand Modeling identifies opportunities for improvement. Whether you need a turnaround that will save your organization or simply to pinpoint what it will take to make your company better, this is a huge benefit. Identifying and remedying problems is how great companies become dominant.

- Measuring and quantifying the intangible aspects of what makes a brand appealing to its most loyal, most profitable customers provides the framework of what you'll need to craft an effective Brand Model.

- Understanding what makes you *you* in your customer's mind reveals what you can change about the way you do business and what aspects of your operation you must never touch.
- Dominant organizations make decisions based upon objective data coupled with insightful analysis—no relying on hunches or blindly trusting the numbers to tell the whole story.
- When a dominant organization finds a formula that works, not only does it stick with that formula, but it puts significant effort and resources into making it work better.

CHAPTER 4

What Is a Brand Model?

There are seamless product launches, and then there's what happened with Apple's iPhone 4.

In the beginning, everything appeared to be going according to plan. There was a great deal of buzz and speculation about what the new iPhone would and wouldn't do. The Apple faithful were eager to upgrade—even before they knew anything about what the latest model would offer. Expectations were high. Enthusiasm was higher.

Then, on what was undoubtedly not the best birthday Apple engineer Gray Powell had ever had, a prototype iPhone 4 was left behind in a bar. It was soon in the possession of Gizmodo, which recognized that it had the tech-blogging scoop of the year on its hands. A PR debacle ensued, with major media outlets speculating first on the veracity of the claim, and then on Apple's efforts to recover the wayward phone, which included the dispatch of California law enforcement officers to break into Gizmodo's offices and seize computer equipment.

Apple eventually recovered the phone, but not before much of the mystique had been stripped away. Anyone with even a passing interest in the new iPhone could get a decent "sneak peek," perhaps on an iPhone 3. This took a lot of the punch out of the iPhone product launch, an area in which Apple usually excels. Analysts have called Apple product launches marketing performance art, and Steve Jobs always played to a packed house.

Despite the shaky start, demand for the new iPhone was strong. PC World, a leading tech blog, issued an "Ultimate Survival Guide" for those who were determined to get an iPhone on June 24, the first day it was available. Customers who wanted to buy their phones at an AT&T store had to have a reservation, and those who wanted to buy at Walmart or Best Buy had to be among the very first in a long line or risk being told, "Sorry, we're out!"

Things were looking good.

Then the first reports detailing the new iPhone's poor connectivity and propensity to drop calls started trickling in. Meredith Vieira, then the *Today* show anchor, shared the story with the nation, awkwardly demonstrating the way iPhone users "should" hold their phone so as to not interfere with the unit's antenna, a posture that was unfortunately completely counter to how anyone would ever hold, much less use, a cell phone.

The story wasn't going to go away. For every Apple fan, there's at least one Apple detractor. Our media cycle is powered by schadenfreude. Nothing will get more airtime than a story that focuses on someone's failing, particularly if the organization doing the failing occupies a dominant position in the marketplace.

The issue—quickly and perhaps inevitably termed AntennaGate—had to be addressed. Steve Jobs had to speak to Apple's fans, particularly those who were less than impressed with the iPhone's performance. There was only one question: what was he going to say?

Modeling for Business

A model's value lies in its ability to predict the future accurately. Models have been used to determine the path of an approaching hurricane, enable cooks to prepare a wide variety of culinary delights, and send space explorers boldly where no man has gone before. Using known data to extrapolate the most likely outcome consistently enables smart, strategic decision making, even in the most dynamic and uncertain of environments.

If there's an environment that's more dynamic and uncertain than the court of public opinion, we don't know what it is. Steve Jobs had to do more than address the iPhone's issues. He had to reassure Apple's fanatically loyal customers that their trust had not been misplaced. He had to reinforce Apple's position as a leading innovator, long the title that the company claimed. With one speech, he had to restore investor confidence and transform a leading story into yesterday's news.

The only way to achieve all of these goals—and make no mistake, all of the goals had to be met; this was not an instance where one could pick and choose achievements—was through the use of modeling. Apple could go forward only with a deep understanding of the needs of all parties to this debacle. Particularly important were the needs of Apple's best customers, a small percentage of fanatically loyal customers that we call *Brand Lovers*.

Apple's success is built squarely on a base of *Brand Lovers*, and Steve Jobs knew this. Apple's dominant position was pretty secure. It enjoyed, and still enjoys, the sweet spot in commerce, where competition is by and large irrelevant. That security hinges, however, on the continued fervor that Apple's customers have for the Apple brand—a larger and more complex relationship than a simple passion for Macs, iPods, iPads, and iPhones.

So when Steve Jobs delivered that speech, he did so knowing that the most valuable ears listening to his words were those attached to his customers' heads. More than to the media, more than to the financial world, and more than to the pundits and prognosticators, Jobs needed to speak directly to his best customers in a way that resonated.

What would resonate with Apple's Brand Lovers? To answer that question, Steve Jobs needed to delve deeply into their psyche. He had to be able to connect with them on a very deep level, moving past a simple discussion of antenna design and complementary bumper guards that would remedy the problem. At issue here were the complex psychological and emotional reactions that Apple's best customers had to the iPhone's disappointing performance.

Jobs's message that day? "We're not perfect." What an extraordinary statement! With these words, Jobs shifted the conversation away from what was wrong with the current incarnation of the iPhone and onto the larger brand issue. By articulating a large part of Apple's appeal to its most loyal customers (the perception of excellence, innovation, and infallibility), and sharing that the company was aware of both that set of expectations and the knowledge that it had fallen short, Jobs was talking directly to Brand Lovers and saying, "We're disappointed too." What had been an adversarial situation was transformed into a community problem, a sorrow shared by the Apple faithful. Jobs also tapped into the deep problem-solving orientation of Apple's best customers by presenting a working stopgap solution to the problem and expressing a commitment to creating an even better solution.

How did he know what to say? It could be that Jobs was a natural marketing genius who could intuitively tap into the deepest, darkest corners of his customers' psyches, with an intimate understanding of what makes them tick. Or, it could be that he used the basic effective and duplicative concepts that go into the tool that dominant companies use to win long term: Brand Modeling.

What Is a Brand Model?

A Brand Model is a complex, highly refined, objective, and scientific analysis of your organization's performance in a wide range of situations, as critical factors of your operation change. Just like a weather forecast, a Brand Model is predictive—it can be used to gain essential insight into how your customer base will respond to changes in the environment. Just like a recipe, a Brand Model identifies and articulates the ingredients necessary for success. Just like the reports that NASA uses to track comets and send satellites deep into the endless night, a Brand Model uses rock-solid data gathered from real-world experiences to reliably extrapolate what will happen when your company enters uncharted waters.

The data that are used to create a Brand Model are more than simple historical facts and figures. While that information is useful, it is only a portion of what business leaders need in order to make informed, strategic decisions. It's essential that you have a deep understanding of why your best customers continue to do business with you. You want to know what motivates them to keep coming back. Why do they recommend your business to their family, their friends, and random strangers that they meet online? A Brand Model decodes the psychological drivers of a brand's best customers, using the insights gathered coupled with historical data to make accurate and actionable predictions of the future.

Building your business around your best customers—the customers who consistently do the most business with you—allows you to strengthen your relationship with those customers. They will do business with you more frequently, and they will buy more from you. Additionally, by refining what makes you more appealing to your best customers, you will attract more customers similar to those who already love you. Increased market share means increased profitability. Building your business around your best customers also eliminates a great deal of risk. By focusing on what works and what your best customers find appealing, you can test concepts before you launch them, making sure that every offering and every initiative you make has a warm reception. The goodwill generated by this approach is so strong and so compelling that it can even overcome organizational missteps, such as Apple's AntennaGate.

The Reasons You Need a Brand Model

If there's one problem that's shared by business leaders in every industry and in every nation, it's the overwhelming lack of certainty. No one knows definitively what will happen tomorrow, yet the ability to glimpse around the corner into the future, and predict with a reasonable degree of confidence what will be found there, is a significant competitive advantage.

Brand Modeling provides business leaders with a measure of certainty, allowing them to assess ahead of time the relative success of their proposed initiatives and campaigns. By providing an absolute framework for decision making, Brand Modeling allows organizational efficiency and the unity of vision that is essential for business success.

That's just the beginning. Brand Modeling has many specific benefits for business leaders, as you'll see later in this chapter.

What Do Your Customers Value the Most?
Identifying Constants

Brand Modeling is measuring the science of branding. Any time you attempt to measure an intangible, you run into difficulty. It's not as if you can pour out a cup of consumer confidence or weigh out a pound of expectations. Brand Modeling, like all forms of market analysis, relies upon the aggregation of anecdotal information, then delving deep into that information to find statistically significant data, correlations, and relationships. The analysis of these data can be used to predict the behavior of your most critical customers: your Brand Lovers, who choose to do business with you consistently, perhaps even exclusively.

By measuring everything that is found to be important, to be absolutely crucial, to your most fervent fans—the absolute fringe of your customer base, the folks who have your logo tattooed on their arms and show up three days in advance of a major sales event so that they can be the first ones through the door—you're getting to the true core of your brand identity. How do your customers see you, and why do they like you so much?

In the simplest terms, we're looking for patterns. What motivates the customer who's been doing business with you for 10 years to keep coming back? Walmart has done extensive research into its customer base and discovered that there are three reasons that are cited as the most important reasons that people shop with them: price, product, and people.

These are Walmart's constants. Every business will have its own unique set of constants. Constants are those characteristics that are the most compelling, powerful reasons that lead customers to do business with you time and time again. People who stay at the Ritz-Carlton always want to be treated like ladies and gentlemen, served by ladies and gentlemen. That's not a desire that's going to go away. The desire for special treatment will always be a major portion of the Ritz's appeal.

Recognizing the unconscious and emotional drivers of consumer behavior is particularly important. At heart, a brand is nothing more than a series of emotional impressions, memories, and aspirations, all tangled up with your logo. These emotional responses are more powerful, and we respond to them more quickly, than more logical, analytical responses. These can be subtle differences. The reasons why a customer feels in alignment with one brand rather than another can be very nuanced. Consider why one family prefers to shop at Target and another at Walmart.

Effective Brand Modeling reveals the nuances, emphasizing those points where your best customers feel the strongest, most meaningful connections with your brand. An analysis of the series of relationships that occur between customers and your brand over the course of many transactions can be done only with a sophisticated, complete, and relevant model—and with such a model, not only can you see tomorrow's opportunities today, but you can position your company to capitalize on them.

Brand Modeling Identifies Opportunities

For years, even decades, commercially produced spaghetti sauce came in one variety: smooth. It was all the same. Sure, there were some flavor variations—Ragu was a little sweeter than Prego, for example—but by and large, the leading manufacturers were racing to be the vendor of choice in a commodity market. Extensive use of rudimentary Brand Modeling—particularly focus groups and test marketing—was critical in helping each manufacturer carve out its own slice of the spaghetti sauce pie, but no one company enjoyed a dominant position. No one company had a differentiator that made its sauce markedly better than the rest.

Prego was desperately seeking that differentiator. It was already using superior ingredients and producing a finer product than its leading competitor, Ragu—but it still lagged behind in market share.

Then Prego started working with Howard Moskowitz. Moskowitz began an experimental process in which he took what had been one of the market's constants—spaghetti sauce must have a smooth texture—and changed it. How would the marketplace respond if the sauce wasn't smooth? Was there a market for spaghetti sauce that included identifiable chunks of cheese, meat, and vegetables?

Prego explored the concept, especially after learning of Moskowitz's research indicating that a third of all spaghetti sauce customers enjoyed chunky sauce. People had never once asked for chunky sauce during the thousands of focus groups that Prego had done previously. However, when chunky sauce was offered as an option, consumer response was great.

It is interesting to examine not only Prego's customers' reactions to the new sauce, but why they felt the way they did. Prego had introduced three types of new sauce. What was it about the chunky variety that resonated so deeply with the spaghetti sauce buyer?

We can look at the societal changes that were taking place at the time, particularly those related to adult women, the primary buyers of Prego. Cultural shifts were prompting a deep, if largely unarticulated, anxiety and fear about the loss of the traditional home and family, particularly iconic traditions such as eating dinner together. Thinner spaghetti sauce may in fact have been more traditional, but the chunky varieties allowed customers to put a meal on the table in a way they found homey and comforting. This sauce was prepared the way they would have done it themselves if they'd had the time and ability to do so. Something as simple as hunks of meat in the spaghetti sauce alleviated feelings of guilt and inadequacy—a sensation that had much to do with Prego's increased market share.

Competitors soon followed suit, but Prego enjoyed a substantial brand boost by essentially creating the chunky sauce category. It was able to attain this position only by listening closely to what its best customers wanted, not only from the company's existing product line, but from the company: what were the expectations being pinned on the Prego brand that had absolutely nothing to do with tomatoes, garlic, and oregano? Once Prego could identify and meet those wants and needs, it enjoyed a much stronger market position. The strength of Brand Modeling lies in the fact that it articulates the intangible expectations and desires your best customers have with regard to your brand—intangibles that you may have been previously unaware of entirely. It is a transformative experience for an organization to realize that it's not in the business of selling tomato sauce. It's selling home and family, tradition, and perhaps an element of self-forgiveness for the cook who feels she's not doing enough for her family.

Zappos tapped into this by realizing that what it sells is not shoes, but a superior customer experience. Life is good has carved out its place in the apparel world by selling optimism. Millions of hotels sell rooms, but the Ritz-Carlton sells pampering.

Can You Trust Brand Modeling?

While the validity of modeling is taken for granted in some fields, it is relatively unknown as a business tool. This raises questions about the mechanism. How trustworthy is Brand Modeling? Is it safe to trust your business's future to this set of statistics?

There are two parts to this question. The first has to do with the ability of anyone, anywhere, to construct a completely accurate predictive model. As of this writing, an absolutely foolproof model doesn't exist for anything. Weather forecasting has come a long way, but no meteorologist anywhere can tell you that he gets everything right every time. Rain falls when the skies were supposed to be sunny, tornadoes form without warning, and the blizzard that school kids were hoping would close school for a week blows right by without leaving a single flake on the ground. It is inevitable that there will be days when the forecast is wrong, but by and large, the model is right an impressive majority of the time.

Models, like the weather forecast, are seldom absolute. We're in the land of probabilities and likelihood here. That does not diminish the utility of a model as a decision-making tool. If the weather forecast says there is a 30 percent chance of rain, do you tell the kids it's time to head for the park? What if it's a 60 percent chance of rain? What if it's 90 percent? A model provides the information you need to make an informed decision.

When the stakes rise, the accuracy of the model goes up in proportion to the emphasis placed on getting accurate information and on analysis and interpretation of those data. Hurricanes are devastating storms. That's why we see the emphasis on being able to track them adequately, complete with an impressive governmental and technological infrastructure devoted to collecting relevant data. There's no point where we can say that we can absolutely predict anything, but there does come a point where the preponderance of the data and the accuracy of analysis approaches certainty.

The same can happen in business. Human behavior is undoubtedly more complex than the patterns of wind, water, and momentum that make up hurricanes. There are more variables to track, and there is the added complexity that consumer behavior is subject to motivations and influences that the customers themselves aren't always fully aware of. More than 90 percent of human behavior is unconscious. It's rare for any of us to be wholly self-aware, even when we're questioned directly. The hardest task for anyone anywhere is to describe why she's doing what she's doing. It's more than possible for an outside, objective observer to discern at least major motivations in individual and group behavior, but to do that for ourselves? It's like trying to lick your elbow.

When your company places greater emphasis and focus on achieving an in-depth understanding of customers' knowledge, an effective and comprehensive Brand Model can indeed be built.

The second part of the question is, can you trust your business to this concept? Can you use the information that modeling provides to offer your customers what they will find most appealing, to step outside of the routine of what organizations have always done in favor of what's going to knock your customers' socks off? Is it safe to stake out a place in the marketplace where you have all the risk and exposure of being a brand like no other?

As much as we hate to do this, we're going to answer a question with a question. Is there any safety inherent in your current decision-making process? How do you know now that the initiatives you're undertaking are the right ones, that the campaign you've just signed off on will resonate with your customer base, or that your next proposed location will welcome your brand with open arms? Organized, filtered, relevant information reduces the level of risk your organization is exposed to. The more you know about your customers, the better able you are to create a model that allows you to eliminate uncertainty. In other words, the more you know, the safer you are, and that's critical, because you need a safe base in order to be innovative, and you need innovation in order to remain viable in today's marketplace.

Where It Counts the Most

- Dominant organizations win because they build their businesses around the wants and needs of their Brand Lovers. In order to focus on your best customers, you need to understand them deeply and concretely. This requires a Brand Model.
- Uncertainty is the biggest challenge that business leaders face. Eliminating uncertainty by using a Brand Model leads to greater profits, increased organizational efficiency, and market dominance.
- A Brand Model articulates and explains the unconscious factors guiding your best customers' purchasing behavior.
- Examining Brand Lovers' behavior patterns reveals constants—those critical aspects of your operation that your best customers value most and that must never be changed.
- Emotional responses to a brand are more powerful and compelling than logical, reasoned responses to a brand. Dominant brands win by focusing on the emotional responses they create within their customers.
- The predictive aspect of Brand Modeling allows you to discern what your customers want now and what they're going to want tomorrow. This "heads-up" is a critical competitive advantage that dominant organizations use to win.
- What are you really selling? Dominant organizations understand that they're selling more than merchandise: they're selling emotional experiences.
- Brand Modeling reveals the expectations your customers have for your organization; this reveals opportunities.

CHAPTER 5

Brand Lovers

Walmart is the world's largest retailer. It has more than 8,000 locations in 15 countries. As many as 1.4 billion people shop at Walmart—every week. Revenue estimates for this undoubtedly dominant company come in at a cool $413.8 billion annually.

Try to find Walmart on the radio, though. It's pretty difficult. For years, it was impossible. There was an extended period of time in which the world's largest retailer didn't have a single radio commercial. It didn't matter where you tuned your dial—country, hip-hop, classic rock, or easy listening—you weren't going to hear a word from Walmart. There wasn't a single jingle, no 20-second spots urging customers to come down to spend less and live better.

Why is that? Sound is an incredibly powerful medium, allowing us to connect with our customers in a direct and meaningful way. Radio is a proven brand builder. It is a tool that many businesses have used to great effect to solidify their market position and increase sales. Surely Walmart, which has demonstrated more than a little business savvy over the years, would want to embrace it.

That's the type of question we just can't leave alone, so we took the next logical step and asked Walmart's leadership what was up. The answer surprised us and reinforced our commitment to the basic premises of Brand Modeling.

Bring On the Brand Lovers

Walmart's chief marketing executive at the time, Paul Higham, had a very simple answer to our question. "We're not on radio," he told us, "because our customers aren't on radio."

While that seemed to be a straightforward enough response, we just couldn't accept it. "How can that be?" was the immediate follow-up question. "You market to everyone."

The answer came faster than Walmart prices fall. "No, we don't. And that's why radio is a bad idea."

Walmart has achieved its dominant position in the marketplace by knowing who—with a frightening degree of precision—its customers are, and who its customers are not. Folk wisdom tells us that appearances can be deceiving, and we have to admit that this is especially true in Walmart's case. It may look as if the mega-retailer is trying to capture every free dollar in the world's marketplace, but the fact is that it has achieved its ongoing profitability by identifying and focusing on the needs of its very best customers—the people we call Brand Lovers. If other people want to shop at its stores, that's fine with Walmart—but at the end of the day, it's all about satisfying its core group of customers.

Not everyone is a Walmart shopper. You probably know people who'd rather cut off their arms than walk past that greeter! Walmart, however, doesn't worry about those people. It focuses its attention and resources on the customers who shop with it regularly, have high average transactions, and have a tendency to encourage others to shop at Walmart. These folks self-identify as hardworking and honest. They are family-focused and great lovers of brand names. If they can purchase a top-name television at a reasonable price, they'll happily do so. For some shoppers, Walmart takes on the role of Robin Hood. The retailer exercises its resources to allow the "average" customer to purchase brand-name items that he otherwise would have no access to.

Walmart makes every decision—from where it opens stores through how much it will pay for merchandise to what product mix to offer at a given location—based on the needs of its Brand Lovers. It researches its best customers intently in order to consistently make the best decisions on their behalf. Walmart knows what its customers want, when they want it, and what they'll pay for it.

Talk about eliminating uncertainty! There is no intuition in Walmart's operating procedure; everything is based on quantifiable data and psychological analysis of its base. We're talking about a vast amount of information that is gathered, analyzed, and used to create what may be the world's leading predictor of customer behavior.

The good news is that this is replicable. Your organization can create the same predictive model based upon your best customers' behaviors. You too can eliminate uncertainty and streamline your company's operations to such a point that you enjoy greater profitability than ever before.

What Makes Walmart's Brand Lovers Love Walmart?

For 19 years, Walmart used the answer to this question as its tagline: "Always Low Prices." It has recently moved on to "Save Money. Live Better"—which still speaks directly to the same point. When you come to Walmart, you know you're not going to wind up spending a lot of money. This is what decades of research has revealed as Walmart's strongest appeal for its best customers. This is what we call a constant—a core value that

Walmart's customers value always, above everything else. If you watch the organization in operation, you'll note that it never really strays too far from that key concept—every aspect of Walmart, from identifying manufacturers and vendors to store layout and construction through branding and marketing, is done with an emphasis on low prices and saving money. It is a continual, unabashed, overt acknowledgment that Walmart is doing all it can to meet its best customers' biggest need.

This may not be subtle, but it's successful. Walmart has no viable competition. According to some studies, more than 80 percent of Americans shop at the mega-retailer at least once during a 12-month period. The majority go far more than once. In a period where even the most optimistic economist would have to admit that things are "challenging," Walmart has experienced growth.

When we want to replicate the level of success that Walmart has had, we have to go through a similar process. Across industries and around the world, dominant brands are changing the way they do business. No longer is ultimate profitability to be found by trying to be all things to all people. Walmart doesn't try to reach everyone. For example, it's not after the high-end home furnishings market. It sells furniture, but these pieces are selected for those customers who have a need to fill and don't want to spend a lot of money filling it. The profit inherent in identifying the most profitable portion of the customer base, delving into its behaviors and motivations, and leveraging that knowledge to better serve existing customers and attract new business far outweighs any potential profit that may exist in efforts to expand the company's offerings into areas that its Brand Lovers don't value.

We realize that this is completely counter to the prevailing wisdom—the approach that tells us that we must position ourselves to be as appealing as possible to as many people as possible in hopes of capturing the greatest part of the market. However, dominant organizations have already abandoned that paradigm, and so should you.

Almost everyone on the planet needs a computer, but not everyone needs a Mac. Apple doesn't even attempt to capture the customer who will fire up his old desktop once a week to send a letter to his local congressman.

Shoes are another basic need, but Zappos is interested only in those customers who want brand-name shoes and superlative customer service. Harley-Davidson doesn't spend any time trying to convert fans of Japanese racing bikes to its brand. It is secure in its knowledge that ultimate profitability comes from serving those customers who avidly want what Harley is already offering.

Finding Your Brand Lovers

Sometimes it is easy to identify people who love your brand. Your best customers have a tendency to let you know they're there. You see them often; they talk about your business online; they're your fans on Facebook and follow you on Twitter. They may even regularly wear apparel emblazoned with your logo. In exceptional cases, an individual may love your organization so much that she has your brand permanently inked into her flesh—that's devotion for you! There's a clear and direct relationship between the level of affection an individual has for your organization and how likely she is to drive six hours and line up at the crack of dawn to attend the opening of a new location. However, a customer's love for your brand doesn't have to be over-the-top all of the time to have a profound effect on your business.

Brand Lovers can look suspiciously normal. You can't necessarily pick them out by sight. There's no secret handshake. It's by their actions that you shall know your Brand Lovers.

When we examine customer behavior, it becomes readily apparent that not all customers act in the same way. We have to impose some order on the data to render them meaningful and actionable. Identifying who your Brand Lovers are means tracking some quantifiable criteria, such as frequency of engagement and typical average sale, and researching the psychological drivers and motivations influencing consumer choices.

Looking at Loyalty: Examining Customer Mindsets

We can start by breaking down consumer mindsets into three basic categories that illuminate the basic motivations behind purchasing behaviors. Every customer engages in all of these behaviors at different points throughout his life. Often, we exhibit all of them within the course of a single day.

When we make decisions logically, thinking through all of the objective criteria, weighing options, and then acting, we're in a *transactional* mindset. You're driving down the road, and you notice that the gas gauge is dipping toward E. You need to get gas as quickly as possible. You'll pull into the next gas station that presents itself, and chances are, if you're presented with two gas stations next to each other, you'll select the one that allows you to save a few cents on every gallon.

Relational mindsets come into play when we make purchasing decisions based upon our feelings. In the aftermath of the BP oil spill, Dawn dish soap, which had a longstanding established relationship with the wild animal rescue community, branded many of its offerings with pictures of animals and the message that a portion of the proceeds would be used to offset the damage to wildlife in the Gulf. Customers responded to the emotional message, further solidifying Dawn's dominant place in the market. Dawn had not changed its formula or done anything else to position itself as the dish soap of choice. Participating in wildlife rescue was nothing new for the brand. It was the decision to raise awareness of Dawn's charitable efforts at a critical time that was such a powerful tool. This was purely an emotional appeal, tying into people's feelings of frustration and longing to do something to alleviate the crisis.

A *loyal* mindset is demonstrated when we make decisions based upon those values and ideals that we hold most deeply. Walmart addresses its customer's strong, compelling urge to provide a high quality of life for the people she loves most despite having limited resources, and it has legions of loyal customers to prove it. We can't overlook the role that emotional connections play in Walmart's success. For many shoppers, Walmart represents "Americana"—a nostalgia-tinged sentiment defined by traditional 1950s values, formed when life seemed simpler. This is a powerful bond.

Not all loyalty is created equal. For most organizations, dealing with the data will reveal that there's a customer loyalty continuum. Individual consumers' engagement can range from Brand Haters (they dislike doing business with you, but do so anyway out of necessity) through the middle ground of Brand Nomads, who can take you or leave you, and Brand Enthusiasts, who are generally favorable toward your organization but have no personal investment in or connection to your brand. Brand Lovers have a demonstrable attachment to and emotional investment in your brand. They like your organization and want you to succeed. More important, they're willing to act in order to see your company thrive.

What This Means to You

If you're committed to growing your business and growing your profitability, all of your marketing and branding efforts must be directed toward creating more Brand Lovers. You must serve your existing Brand Lovers better than anyone else. The road to ultimate profitability can be taken only when you put your Brand Lovers in the driver's seat and let them take the wheel.

This means going the extra mile for those customers who are doing that little bit more to keep your business thriving and growing. This is the critical differentiation that will help you stand out in the mind of your audience. You're making your Brand Lovers feel special—and in a world where there's nothing as rare as individual attention, this is an irresistible attractant that will build strong customer bonds.

Back in the early days of the World Wrestling Federation (now known as WWE), there were free meatball subs on hand for the audience members. The concept is scalable. Dave's Soda and Pet City, a four-store specialty pet retail chain in Massachusetts, uses annual apple pies and car-wash coupons for his best customers to bring them back to his store, rather than to the nearby PetSmarts, Petcos, and other larger competitors. Serving your Brand Lovers better than anyone else moves your business to a point where competition becomes irrelevant—because no one else does what your organization is doing.

When the skateboarding community began to favor the unique sneakers made by the Vans company, Vans responded by focusing all of its efforts on understanding and filling the footwear (and later apparel) needs of skateboarders. Today, Vans is a flagship brand of the VFC Corporation, which reported $7.2 billion in revenues last year.

Losing for Love?

If we conduct our business in such a way that we're providing better service to our Brand Lovers—which includes, among other things, refining our marketing, services, and operations to reflect what they value most—what will happen to our relationships with the rest of our customers? There's a great deal of fear out there that taking a targeted path toward excellence will alienate our existing customer base, driving a great wedge into relationships that weren't great to begin with and sending former business running off into the arms of the nearest competitor.

We must counter those fears with a dose of reality. First of all, your Brand Nomad customers—those that you see only sporadically and that have virtually no bond with your company—are already spending a fair amount of time with your competition. This isn't a game you're currently winning, but it could be.

Your efforts to better serve the needs of your Brand Lovers may have a positive impact on your Brand Nomads. Something as simple as a change in store hours designed specifically in response to Brand Lovers' input can also appeal to other customers. The change might be so important that a Brand Nomad finds himself considering your company more favorably, to the point where he might become a Brand Enthusiast or even a Brand Lover. You may lose a few individuals along the way, but if you examine the growth patterns of dominant companies— IKEA, Apple, and perhaps especially Walmart—the numbers consistently show that growth outpaces loss.

Focusing on your Brand Lovers will also increase your overall market share. As you're improving the relationship you have with the majority of your customer base—ideally transforming nomads and enthusiasts into lovers—you also are creating buzz and excitement around your brand that will attract new business. Some of these customers will become Brand Lovers, while some may establish only a nomad-level relationship with your business. You will see your existing customers more frequently and establish relationships with new customers.

Virgin Mobile competes very effectively in the competitive cell phone marketplace—an environment teeming with schools of haters and nomads—because it doesn't require a contract. This point of differentiation—strategically positioning itself against what Brand Haters hated most about the brands they were currently doing business with—gave Virgin a great opportunity to create Brand Lovers.

Brand Lovers Are Your Most Profitable Customers

It's important that you understand who your Brand Lovers are. It's critical that you understand what they do for your organization.

Your Brand Lovers are your pillars of profitability. They are ultimately responsible for your success or failure as an organization. The more Brand Lovers you have, and the more you understand and respond to what drives them, the more dominant your company will be.

Brand Lovers are highly responsive to your marketing efforts, are predisposed to recommend your products and services to others, and are loyal, frequent customers. They have more impact on your bottom line than any other existing or potential customer group you may have access to.

This plays out in two ways. First and foremost, loyal customers do more business with you. Transforming just 10 percent of your occasional customers—Brand Enthusiasts, for example, or even Brand Nomads—into Brand Lovers can radically change your financial picture. In a large company, we're talking about billions of dollars in additional revenue and radically higher profit margins.

Amazon.com CEO Jeff Bezos said it very well when he explained, "We take those funds that might be used to shout about our service, and put those funds instead into improving the service. That's the philosophy we've taken from the beginning. If you do build a great experience, customers tell each other about that. Word of mouth is very powerful."

Profitability is also enhanced because understanding the wants and needs of your Brand Lovers allows you to work smarter, not harder. You can identify and focus on those efforts and initiatives that are most likely to offer a great return. Your knowledge of your Brand Lovers means that you can build a stronger, more distinct, and more appealing brand, strategically differentiated within the marketplace.

Articulating a fully realized customer profile makes it easier and more affordable to acquire new customers—and subsequently leverage the higher-order psychological needs, such as esteem and personal growth, that are shared by your best customers in order to keep them.

This plays out in less theoretical terms. Walmart's leadership strives to identify needs before they are manifested—the ultimate in customer service. No sooner do storm clouds start to congregate over the Gulf of Mexico than cases of water, Pop-Tarts, and batteries take center stage in local Walmarts—where they sell out at blinding speed.

This growth in market share takes place alongside a corresponding increase in vision and confidence. Wasteful mistakes and off-target initiatives and campaigns are avoided. The focus on eliminating uncertainty means establishing a knowledge bank of what works for your best customers, giving you a range of tried-and-true marketing tools that will only reinforce and strengthen existing profitable relationships.

Why Are Brand Lovers So Profitable?

What's so special about Brand Lovers? What are the characteristics that render this group of customers so profitable? There are three criteria that must be met: frequency, retention, and word of mouth. Together, these components make up the trifecta of awesome. The Brand Lover is a loyal, highly profitable customer who loves to tell others about your organization.

Brand Lovers Do a Lot of Business with You

The first measure we look for is frequency, which refers to how often your customers do business with you. What we're looking for here is a relatively high rate of engagement—the Starbucks faithful, who stop every day on the way to the office, for example. We can also examine frequency in terms of purchase size. Among Walmart's frequent shoppers, some spend $50 a week and others $500. Your Brand Lovers do a high level of business with you often and consistently.

It has been said that an existing customer is five times more likely to buy from you than a new prospect. As an added bonus, you already have an established relationship with your Brand Lovers. You don't have to sell them on who you are, what you do, or how fantastic your service is. They're already sold. They're believers. Your Brand Lovers will return to your business time and time again, rewarding your organization with higher frequency of business and greater wallet share, both per engagement and over the long term. The cultivation of this growth is a great untapped opportunity for many businesses.

This brings us to one of the fundamental concepts required for business success. Customer loyalty is a better determinant of profitability than mass appeal. It is a better approach, from both a strategic and an efficiency perspective, to structure a business that appeals to the loyal cadre of Brand Lovers who are your most profitable customers than to try to engage the interest of the market as a whole.

Your Brand Lover Is Loyal

Retention is the next factor to take into account. Once a customer begins a relationship with you, how long does it last? Your Brand Lovers are those who are loyal to your brand. They prefer you over similar businesses. When they're in the market for your product or service, they come to you first. Few companies achieve dominance by working with a customer only once. True profitability lies in recognizing and maximizing the lifetime value of the customer.

Apple puts a significant portion of its marketing efforts into the retention part of the equation. The Genius Bar and the popular Apple Classes educate and empower its customers to get full value from their purchases, an effort that Mac lovers reward with fanatical loyalty.

Harley-Davidson, in addition to its extensive efforts supporting the Harley Owners Group, throws tremendous anniversary celebrations, attracting bikers from around the world who gather simply for the joy of being with one another. MINI has followed suit, fostering the same type of community among fans of its distinctive small cars with yearly events.

The most compelling measure has to be customer behavior. Your Brand Lovers will choose to do business with you more often than they will do business with your competitors. Their love means that you're their number one choice, their go-to option, their default setting.

There are no options. When you are in this position, you have no relevant competition. This can even develop into an "us versus them" phenomenon, where Brand Lovers identify with a company so strongly that they perceive the company's competitors as adversaries. Dominant companies—those that we call Cult Brands—promote personal freedom, a heady message that Brand Lovers don't let go of easily. Brand Lovers place such a high value on this sense of community that it has a significant impact on their purchasing behaviors. A Mac user won't suddenly "switch sides" and embrace a PC. Harley owners don't go to rallies on a Kawasaki, and in many homeowners' eyes, nothing runs like a John Deere.

The fact that your Brand Lovers will choose your organization over all others is a critical factor in helping your organization achieve a dominant position within your industry.

Brand Lovers Tell Everyone About You

Brand Lovers believe that a joy shared is a joy increased. They enjoy telling others about your business, and they are active in enlarging your customer base. There is no sales tool as powerful as a personal recommendation from a friend, and Brand Lovers are great at making recommendations. Basically, we're talking about the source of your positive word of mouth.

Dominant brands understand that they have to give their best customers something truly wonderful, something that they can talk about in a world that places a high value on information. When Netflix came on the scene, few industry insiders thought the start-up had a realistic chance against the movie rental industry's dominant player, namely Blockbuster. However, Netflix customers—who greatly enjoyed the convenience of never having to return a DVD to the store in time to avoid a late fee and the infinite selection that Netflix offered—found great benefit in the start-up's services. Not only did they find a benefit for themselves, but they found a benefit so great that they couldn't resist telling their friends about it.

This is better than gold. You could say that we're hardwired to share stories with one another. In our earliest days as a species, this was a survival mechanism. Today, the "inside information" on what's new, great, and not to be missed plays a critical role in our social lives. Those individuals who have that knowledge gain valuable social capital. They gain status among their peer group. Their relationship with your organization—no matter how tangential—helps them define themselves in their own eyes and in the eyes of their peers.

Netflix did it right. It gave its customers something positive to talk about, and talk about it they did. In response, the little company that didn't have a single physical location was soon outperforming its competitors. Blockbuster did its best to emulate a similar strategy, shedding slow-performing brick-and-mortar locations, but it wasn't enough to keep the chain from having to file for bankruptcy. Understanding what movie renters wanted most enabled Netflix to change the industry, and that change was borne on a tidal wave of customer-generated word of mouth.

You don't have to provide any incentive or solicit this commentary. In fact, it may be better if you don't. When Brand Lovers share their enthusiasm naturally and organically, their words are considered more sincere and meaningful than anything an organization can generate on its own behalf. In fact, attempts to manipulate the word-of-mouth stream can elicit mistrust and shatter the hard-won bonds of customer loyalty.

Your Brand Lovers are playing an important role for you here. Customers will talk about only what they find to be exceptional. It's a reverse-engineering sort of approach to discovering what their baseline expectations are. The more you know about what your best customers take for granted, the easier it becomes to discover what it will take to knock their socks off. Netflix found late fees, and won. The same opportunity exists for your organization—if you're willing to listen to and focus on your Brand Lovers.

Where It Counts the Most

- Brand Lovers are your most loyal, most enthusiastic, and most profitable customers.
- Abandon the paradigm that says that your company should try to be all things to all people. Success depends on identifying what you do best and what your Brand Lovers cherish about you, and delivering more of that.
- Brand Lovers are defined by their actions. They do lots of business with you, actively promote your company to their family and friends, and actively look for a way to connect with your brand.
- Loyalty is created when we find brands whose values and ideals are in alignment with our own. Dominant organizations know their Brand Lovers' values and ideals and act accordingly.
- Dominant organizations win by serving the wants and needs of their Brand Lovers better than any other organization. The Brand Lovers are in the driver's seat. Their wants, needs, and desires guide the company's directions.
- Look for opportunities to serve your Brand Lovers that are unique in your industry. Dare to do what no one else is doing. Going the extra mile for your Brand Lovers pays rich reward. Customers value individual attention, feeling part of the group, and receiving tangible rewards.
- Knowing what attracts your Brand Lovers makes it easier to attract more like-minded customers, naturally growing your customer base and market share.
- To find your Brand Lovers, analyze sales data, conduct in-person interviews, and pay attention to social media. You'll see the same types of people cropping up time and time again.

- Brand Lovers are motivated by authentic, sincere emotions. Resist the temptation to interfere or manufacture their enthusiasm: nothing wrecks brands faster than the impression that they're "gaming" the public.

PART III

Building Your Brand Model

CHAPTER 6

Uncovering Your Brand's Core

Modeling provides the answers and the direction that we're looking for. It is the ideal tool for eliminating uncertainty and improving your overall business performance. Now we get to the critical point: what are you modeling your brand around?

You can model your brand around any number of elements. It's certainly possible to model your business based on industry standards, analyzing and emulating the behaviors and practices of your peer group. This is a conservative approach that offers at least the appearance of security. The major drawback to this approach is that it offers organizations no path to move beyond mediocrity. If you are doing what everyone else is doing, you are essentially denying yourself the opportunity to stand out from the crowd.

More than a few organizations have modeled themselves directly on the competition. You don't have to question many theme park and amusement industry officials before you start hearing about Disney. How many luxury watch companies aspire to be Rolex? How many upscale car manufacturers want to be Mercedes?

How many of these wannabe anythings can you name off the top of your head? There you see the problem with this approach. While there are obvious advantages to learning from what your competition does well, modeling your organization around a competitor's practices cannot give you a distinct, individual identity in the marketplace. Unless you're content with branding yourself as a cheaper alternative to what the customer truly desires, this is generally not the best route to achieving a dominant industry position.

We believe that there is only one intelligent choice to make at this juncture. Modeling your business based upon your best customers—your Brand Lovers—is the only sure route to success. All of the excellent brands we've mentioned throughout this book (and those we've left out!) do this, whether they're aware of it or not. Apple, Harley-Davidson, IKEA, and Walmart: they are where they are because they build their organization centered on their Brand Lovers.

Building on Our Strengths: Why Brand Lovers Are Important

Why should we model our businesses based on our best customers' behavior?

We know that our Brand Lovers are our most profitable customers. That's critical, because there are only two routes that an organization can take to sustainably increase its growth. The first route comes from selling more to its existing loyal customer base. That can mean brand extensions, or expanding the number and variety of products and services that your Brand Lovers can purchase from you. It can mean strategically targeted campaigns to put you in your best customers' minds during slow points in the business cycle—one extra engagement per year per customer has a transformative impact on any organization's bottom line. It can mean many things, but the only way you're going to know what will make your Brand Lovers buy more is to know what makes your Brand Lovers buy in the first place.

The second route to profitability involves expanding the ranks of Brand Lovers that your organization has. Identifying and attracting more individuals who will embrace your company enthusiastically has an immediate and obvious positive impact. The benefits increase when you have the knowledge to not only attract these new customers, but also retain them. Relying on what has been proven to attract and keep your most profitable customers is a good starting point.

Ultimate profitability comes when you combine the two approaches. Better serving the needs of your Brand Lovers will create the enthusiasm and buzz necessary to attract new customers to your brand. There's a cyclical pattern that builds on itself. It begins by knowing who your best customers are, and what makes them love your company.

What happens if you don't have this knowledge? It's like trying to cook without a recipe. You might wind up with a great dish purely by chance, but it's more likely that you're cooking up a big batch of disaster stew.

Kmart's Catastrophe

Look at Kmart. As one of the first entrants in the discount marketplace, Kmart had built a strong brand for itself and commanded a pretty decent market share. Fundamental to Kmart's success was the never-articulated but well-understood premise that customers would enjoy lower prices, but that they'd also be getting far less in the way of a shopping experience, customer service, and merchandise quality.

This worked for a while, but then Kmart made the classic mistake. It assumed that all of its customers were happy and satisfied. It even ignored the warning signs: increasing customer complaints about slow service, empty shelves, and subpar shopping experiences. When Walmart came on the scene, offering the same low prices *and* great service, Kmart lost customers in droves. They had not been given a compelling reason to stay. No effort had been put into keeping healthy customer relationships strong. No energy had gone into keeping Kmart's Brand Lovers happy.

Brand Modeling provides us with a way to achieve organizational wellness. It's both a diagnostic tool, used to pinpoint problems as they arise, and a prescriptive tool, giving us the information we need to keep our Brand Lovers in optimal health.

Identifying Brand Lovers

Modeling your business around the wants and needs of your Brand Lovers requires first identifying who your Brand Lovers are and then discerning their wants and needs in great detail.

This is a two-step process. The first step uses objective, quantifiable data to pinpoint your best customers. After that, it's time to delve into your Brand Lovers' psyches in order to better understand the bond they have with your organization.

Defining Your Brand Lovers

There are three parameters we need to consider when identifying Brand Lovers: retention, frequency, and word of mouth. A Brand Lover will exhibit all three qualities, having done a great deal of business with you over the course of a period of time and happily sharing his positive view of your company with others.

Each organization will have to set its own parameters for defining a Brand Lover. The criteria used can include attitudes toward the brand, total annual purchases, frequency of store visits, willingness to recommend the brand to friends and family, and presence on and contribution to company social media sites and online forums, among others.

Your pool of Brand Lovers can be quite broad. Harley-Davidson, for example, has a wide range of Brand Lovers—people who identify with the company even though they've yet to purchase a bike. They may demonstrate this love by purchasing Harley-themed apparel, attending Harley events, or regularly window-shopping at the local dealership.

One of the most ardent Harley-Davidson Brand Lovers we ever met worked at Coca-Cola. He was a proud member of HOG (the Harley Owners Group), even though he didn't have a bike. His entire retirement plan—everything he was working endless hours for now—was centered on retiring and spending his golden years on the open road. It didn't matter that he didn't have that Harley now. He was going to have it soon.

Identifying this man as a Brand Lover and discerning how many other Brand Lovers like him exist, who are about to retire and want to embrace the Harley lifestyle, can potentially drive millions in sales.

Brand DNA

Identifying your Brand Lovers is the first step. The next task is to learn everything you can about them. Effective Brand Modeling requires more than a cursory knowledge of your customer base. The old adage that appearances can be deceiving is nowhere more applicable than it is here. Countless catastrophic business decisions have been made based upon surface-level understanding of a customer base.

It's imperative that you delve deeper and understand more to fully grasp not only who your customers are, but why they act the way they do. You need a complex, nuanced understanding of your Brand Lovers, especially their motivations and what underlies their relationship with your organization.

Doing this requires examining what we call your Brand DNA. Think of Brand DNA as the genetic code that dictates the relationship between your Brand Lovers and your organization. Brand DNA identifies both the variables that create strong bonds and the nonnegotiable points of connection that Brand Lovers insist upon, as well as opportunities for growth and brand differentiation.

The DNA that each of us carries around within our genes is composed of four different nucleotides, each distinct and each critically important. These nucleotides are arranged time and time again in a long chain. Each strand is a unique combination that contributes directly to our identity, defining our very self.

In the same way, Brand DNA consists of four variables, humanistic drivers, archetypal images, cultural stories, and emotional connections, that forge the brand's identity and define its place in the customer's mind.

Humanistic Drivers

Suppose a distant relative of yours dies, leaving you a surprise inheritance of $2 million. Being the sensible, prudent person that you are, you decide to put at least some of this windfall away for a rainy day. Where are you going to stow the cash?

Will you opt for your local credit union, owned and run by people you know? Or will you opt for a national chain, such as HSBC or Bank of America? The larger chains offer their customers better interest rates and nicer perks, but based on the data that only 16 percent of HSBC customers believe that the company consistently acts in their best interests, a feeling shared by a third of Bank of America customers, the credit union option may turn out to be overwhelmingly attractive.

Why?

It turns out that there are things in this world that are more important than logic. Chief among these are humanistic drivers. Humanistic drivers are the innate, often unconscious and unarticulated needs that we all share. Our need to generate profit with that $2 million may be significantly less than our need for security, to know that our money is safe and protected.

Before someone is a customer, she's a person, and people have needs. These needs motivate us, guiding our behavior in profound ways. They are imperatives, things that we have to do; if we fail to do them, for whatever reason, we'll continue trying to fulfill them.

Understanding what these unconscious humanistic drivers that propel our customers' behaviors are allows us to understand what role we're filling in their lives that transcends the immediately obvious. Any car will fulfill the need for transportation, but the MINI Cooper fills a need for belonging and self-expression in a way that's distinct and appealing to its Brand Lovers.

Can I Get an Upgrade?

Humanistic drivers are seldom acknowledged or articulated by our Brand Lovers. Who goes to Starbucks saying, "Today, I'm going to honor my need for belonging and social validation with a caffeinated beverage"? Not many people. It requires insight and analysis to identify the specific humanistic drivers that are most at play in your Brand Lovers' perception of your brand.

There is a universal aspect to humanistic drivers. Everyone experiences these needs, but we each have our own beliefs that help us determine the best way to meet them. Since the dawn of time, people have been guided by one overwhelming principle: the desire to replace their current set of circumstances with something better. We're always hungry for more—a bigger house, a better car, the best cell phone. We live to upgrade our existence. The market has been built on providing specific examples of what bigger, better, and best mean.

Maslow's hierarchy gives us a little bit more structure to work with. Maslow arranged human needs into multiple categories, each one predicated on having all the needs that come before it met first. Everyone has biological and physical needs—shelter, food, water, warmth, sex, sleep, and air to breathe. It's only after those needs are satisfied that we can move on to higher-level needs: safety, belonging, esteem, and cognitive. Fulfilling those needs positions an individual to evolve even further, manifesting as the need for beauty, self-actualization, and transcendence.

From our perspective, we need to focus on how biological drivers guide and energize the satisfaction that Brand Lovers get from engaging with our brand. We have to understand our customers' needs from a humanistic point of view. We can't reduce them to demographic drones. You can't sell to a 35-year-old Hispanic male from Atlanta who makes $85,000 with the same precision or effectiveness as you can create a Brand Lover, but identifying and selling to your Brand Lovers requires understanding your customer as a whole person, one who can't be defined as a single category, but who instead has a range of complex needs.

If you want to see this being done exceptionally well, go to your nearest Apple store. The minute you step inside the place, you'll notice that it is different from any other type of store you've been in. You won't find a single scrap of conventional retail design here.

There are no narrow aisles threading between shelves packed with merchandise. Wide-open spaces are decorated with inviting workstations. There are no cash registers. There's nothing small anywhere in the store—oversized images are visible from every point in the room. Along one wall stands a bar, staffed with people who seem absolutely thrilled to show you how to make your computer do everything you want it to, and six things you didn't even know were possible.

These stores are, on a square foot basis, among the most profitable retail locations in the world. This is partly because Apple has strategically and consistently focused on meeting its customers' lower-level needs, particularly belonging—witness the Mac vs. PC Guy commercials—esteem, and knowledge. It has shifted away from selling technology to giving people the tools they need in order to be great. The customer reaction to having this unarticulated need met, and met well, has been strong, widespread, and enduring. Customers buy Macs, iPhones, iPods, iPads—you name it. But that's not what Apple's selling.

No Secret in the Secret Recipe

The urge, of course, is to deconstruct what Apple's doing. What's its magic? What is it doing right, and can we do it ourselves?

It's the same feeling we get in a restaurant when the waiter brings us a magnificent dessert, perhaps a chocolate soufflé. We see the majestic puff, rich and dark and chocolate, dusted with the perfect amount of confectioner's sugar, with three raspberries and mint leaves garnishing the whole. Surely some alchemy went into this delicious treat—and being curious, we go into the kitchen to investigate how the chef works her magic.

That's where it's revealed that this sublime dessert, this transcendent soufflé, is nothing more than eggs, cocoa, sugar, and air, garnished at the last possible moment before it reaches your table.

Are you disappointed? Does your pleasure in the soufflé diminish? That's where the magic kicks in, and this is where Apple excels. Its approach is not secretive. It's managed to be about as overt as you can be without painting, "This is what we're doing" in foot-high letters on the wall in red spray paint. Apple aficionados know that they're buying into a lifestyle of creativity and aesthetic sensibility. They know that they're being offered a chance to belong to a select club. They know that they're paying premium prices for a premium experience. They have the ingredients of the Apple approach laid out in front of them from the minute they walk through the door. Apple has identified and focuses on meeting its customers' needs. It's as simple, and as complex, as that.

And they eat it up. It's the chocolate soufflé again. Even when you know how it's made, it's still good. No secret recipe is required.

You Don't Win Silver, You Lose Gold: The Power of Archetypal Images

The year 1996 was an interesting year for Nike. Having the Olympic Games in Atlanta was a potential marketing bonanza for the company, which, after all, sells athletic shoes to athletic people who are aligned with the Olympic spirit.

Nike hit the ground running. Atlanta was blanketed with billboards. The company bought spot ads from NBC in the top 20 markets, saturating the airwaves. In addition to the "You don't win silver, you lose gold" line that earned the company the lasting animosity of the International Olympic Committee, it used the following slogans:

Pageantry is a distraction.
I'm not here to trade pins.
Contempt is a hundredth of a second.

It doesn't take much to discern Nike's message: winning is everything. "If I say I'm just thrilled to compete," one ad told audiences, "blame my interpreter."

We have an innate competitive drive, a biological need to outperform others and win the big prize. Survival of the fittest started for our species on the very first day. The healthiest, strongest, and smartest survived, making them nature's winners. Nike, named for the Greek goddess of victory, taps into that drive by giving its customer base an easily identifiable way to meet it: wear our shoes and be the victor!

The easily identifiable way to meet a need, a pattern of behavior, can be represented by an archetypal image. The eminent psychoanalyst Carl Jung was one of the first to notice that humans have instinctual behaviors. Those behaviors come in patterns, and he called those patterns *archetypes* because they represented a blueprint for how humans have been expressing their instincts for two million years.

So if we have an instinct to win, we can take on the role of the victorious warrior. Setting aside American Gladiators, we don't have a whole lot of actual victorious warrior action going on in our culture, so we substitute the next best thing. Athletes are our de facto warriors. We've come from Spartacus to Shaq.

When we want to be victorious, we emulate others who are. We use their behavior as a model to guide our own. We strive to take on aspects of that archetype for ourselves. One easy way to do this—to become Shaq or, to quote another Nike campaign, to Be Like Mike—is to wear the same shoes that these star athletes endorse.

Nike is perhaps the most consistently effective company at using archetypal imagery in its marketing. It has continually, over the years, come back to the same message: its shoes are the shoes of victors, of warriors, of the triumphant few.

Clearly identifying the archetypal images that appeal most to your customer base brings you that much closer to being able to satisfy your Brand Lovers consistently. These images resonate with your Brand Lovers on a fundamental, visceral level. They give your customers a reason to say, "Yes, this is for me!" by providing a pattern of behavior that is in alignment with the way your Brand Lovers behave or would like to behave.

When Nike evokes the victorious warrior, it shows more than an athlete at a moment of triumph. It expands and capitalizes on that concept, showing the athlete demonstrating determination, courage, resilience, and other attributes integral to becoming that victorious warrior.

Nike has shown not only the warrior triumphant, but the warrior engaged in battle, such as the campaign featuring 2007 Paralympian Matt Scott, who plays basketball from his wheelchair. Other campaigns have featured athletes who are facing an enormous challenge or a seemingly insurmountable obstacle—endless miles of uphill road to run or defensive linemen so big they need their own zip code. There are multiple points where customers can identify with the warrior concept. Even if they're not victorious right now, they're determined that they're going to win eventually.

The power of the archetype can be aspirational as well as realized. These images appeal because they show us not only where we are, but where we want to be. They represent who we are when we envision our best selves.

Identifying Your Brand's Archetypal Images

The next step in the Brand-Modeling process is to determine what archetypes your Brand Lovers associate with your organization. You want to discover what types of mental images come to mind when your Brand Lovers think about your company.

Your Brand Lovers may give you a wide range of answers. Some of these answers may be immediately obvious and appealing to you, but others may be total surprises. Always remember that your brand is not what *you* think it is, but what your customers' perception of it is.

Nike's victorious warrior is one archetype. There are countless universal figures that will be expressed, in a wide range of ways, by your Brand Lovers. Other universal figures include the nurturing parent, the technological wizard, and the free spirit. A single word can spur dozens of associations and images in your customers' minds. Collecting insight from a significant sample of your best customers will give you a mass of data: images, descriptions, and personifications of your brand, all from the customer's point of view.

Sorting through and analyzing these data will allow you to identify patterns and frequently appearing images. This reveals which archetypes are most dominant and relevant to your brand. Pinpointing the most prevalent and powerful archetypes associated with your brand gives you the information you need to create points of alignment between your organization and your best customers.

Cultural Stories

Out west, the skies go on forever, wide and blue. The sun shines over a rugged landscape filled with challenges, but nothing that can't be overcome by a strong, rugged man, a man who is often silent but always ready to step up and do what needs doing. The type of man who conquered the frontier, who embraces adventure and lives life to the fullest.

In short, the Marlboro man. Complete with iconic black cowboy hat and a scarily square jaw, the Marlboro man is recognized around the world as an emblem of manly individualism and adventure.

What leads smokers to select Marlboros? A significant part of the reason comes from what the brand represents to them. Marlboro has provided a compelling narrative with a story that is both familiar and appealing to its base. There's nothing inherently adventurous about smoking (setting aside the perpetual carcinogenic crapshoot, of course), but lighting up allows Marlboro smokers to tap into the tale and fulfill their own longing for the wide-open frontier.

Cultural stories are tools that we as a society have developed for a specific purpose. These tales teach us ways to resolve the conflicts and internal tensions that plague our existence. They provide a mechanism for problem solving, acting as a guide that we can use when making our own decisions. These cultural stories are powerful examples, especially since they often incorporate the archetypal images that we can identify with on a personal level.

In other words, cultural stories teach people how to act when they're being their ideal selves. They are symbolic road maps that we use to navigate our way through life, strategic touchstones to refer to as we move forward from where we are to where we want to be. Cultural stories provide the framework we see ourselves in, both as individuals and in relationship to others.

Cultural stories come in a range of sizes. National identity is a rich source of cultural stories. To be an American means having ownership in the tales of George Washington crossing the Delaware, the California gold prospectors, and everyday fairy tales like the Three Little Pigs (that is, building a strong home). On the other end of the scale, we have family-sized cultural stories, in which our ancestors' actions can be used not only to guide us through contemporary challenges, but to define who we are. Every organization has its own set of cultural stories. Dominant organizations know how to leverage these narratives into compelling messages that resonate deeply with their Brand Lovers.

Identifying Your Organization's Cultural Stories

To identify your organization's cultural stories, you need to talk to your best customers about the experiences they have with your brand. You want to know what experiential aspects of the brand engagement remain with your customers after the fact. What do they remember? What remains as an important memory?

What's the best part of going to Disneyland? You'd better believe that the people at Disney pay close attention to that question because the answer plays a critical role in shaping the narrative that Disney presents to its audience. Stories of personal celebrations held within the park, for example, contributed to one of Disney's most successful initiatives, in which customers are urged to celebrate life's major events—birthdays, true love, reunions, and triumphs—at the park.

Again, as with the archetypes, you'll discover a range of individual stories. People love to tell stories about their experiences, and the stronger the bond, the more intense the stories will be. Not only do these stories reinforce the bond that our Brand Lovers have with us, but they attract others to investigate the brand because they want to have the same experience. They want to have their own tales to tell.

There is a peril here. Often, organizations rush directly from identifying a cultural story to transforming it into a tagline. We must do more than identify these stories. We must understand them in their entirety first, placing them in perspective in the context of our Brand Lover's life, and discerning why they're important, when they're important, and how important they are relative to the other cultural stories and influences that are at play in our Brand Lover's life. This will allow us to position our organizations in the most relevant, appropriate fashion.

Your Place in History

An important function of your brand's cultural stories is to tell the tale of your brand's history. We have here the totality of what your best customers associate with your organization, the accumulation of imagery, color, and personifications that define you in their mind.

This is a critical guiding tool to rely upon when making business decisions. It's always best to brand with history in mind. If you look back over 100 years' worth of Harley-Davidson culture, you're going to see lots of black, lots of orange, and lots of eagle wings and shield logos. It would take tremendous force to shift the Brand Lovers' image of Harley away from this iconography and onto something else, and why would you want to? Brand Modeling provides us with the proof of what works and serves as an admonition that if it's not broke, don't fix it!

Mind you, this isn't always a lesson that gets through. Harley made its own misstep during its 100th anniversary celebration, booking Elton John as its headline performer. Elton John may have lots of fans, but in the context of a HOG rally, he's far off the mark. The performance went over like a chromed balloon, to almost no one's surprise.

Someone among Harley's leadership made a fundamental mistake. You can't give Brand Lovers what you think they'll enjoy. You have to give them what they tell you they enjoy, while simultaneously anticipating their future needs. As Steve Jobs said in an interview with *BusinessWeek* (May 25, 1998), "It's really hard to design products by focus groups. A lot of times, people don't know what they want until you show it to them." To know your brand, you have to know your customers.

Emotional Targets

Ultimately, you're searching for the emotional connections your best customers get from engaging with your brand. When a brand is operating at its best, it becomes adept at provoking complex, consistent emotional reactions in its Brand Lovers. These emotional reactions are so powerful, so pleasing, and so compelling to the brand's customers that they seek them out time and again.

Examining the relationships among humanistic drivers, archetypal images, and cultural stories provides an insight into how the customer perceives your brand. The emotional targets details the why. What is the desired outcome that your best customers seek when they come to your stores, visit your website, and do business with you?

Customers who head to Whole Foods may be in need of carrot juice, flaxseed, and a chicken that never had to endure a cage before it became an entrée, but what they want, what drives them to select Whole Foods rather than any of a dozen other grocery stores, is the availability of fresher produce, meats, and dairy raised organically, along with a sense of social responsibility, personal accountability, cultural change, and self-satisfaction that form the backbone of the chain's emotional message. Whole Foods is committed to taking care of the world around it, using its business to create positive change in the world. The chance to be part of that change provides a powerful emotional connection to its Brand Lovers. Carrot juice is carrot juice is carrot juice, but carrot juice that makes you feel like you're doing your part to save the world? That makes all the difference, and that makes the Whole Foods brand.

Where It Counts the Most

- Brand Modeling affords organizations two routes to profitability. Encouraging Brand Lovers to do even more business with you is the first; swelling the ranks of your best customers is the second.
- Better serving the needs of your best customers will make your organization more appealing to like-minded customers who may have been only vaguely interested before. Soon, you'll have more Brand Lovers.
- Having loyal customers is never enough. Dominant organizations continually take active steps to keep their best customers happy.
- Pay attention to customer complaints. If you don't, some other organization will, and it will leverage those points of opportunity as a way to lure away your customer base.
- Identifying Brand Lovers who haven't yet been able to purchase your products and services and giving them a way to connect with your brand can increase revenues and brand equity.
- Dominant organizations win by identifying and meeting the most compelling needs motivating their Brand Lovers.
- Archetypal images represent powerful, compelling, universal concepts that are part of every human's experience. Clearly identifying the archetypal images that hold the most power for your best customers deepens your understanding of your most profitable customers and provides you with one of the tools you need to be able to communicate with them more effectively.
- Every country, company, and social group will have its own set of cultural stories. Dominant organizations win by identifying the cultural stories that are most compelling to their best customers, and leveraging that knowledge to create effective messaging.

- Your company's history is a rich source of cultural stories. Iconography and imagery that have been associated with your organization for years have a weight and a meaning all their own.
- Remember, it's all about the Brand Lovers. Never assume that you know what's meaningful to them. Ask them. Listen to what they tell you.

CHAPTER 7

Generating Insights and Discovering Meaning

Every morning, a gazelle wakes up. It knows that it must run faster than the fastest lion, or it will be killed. Every morning, a lion wakes up. It knows that it must run faster than the slowest gazelle, or it will starve to death. It doesn't matter whether you're a lion or a gazelle—when the sun comes up, you'd better be running.

What makes the gazelle run? What spurs the lion to run ever faster? Instinctive forces are at play, driving every step and providing the impetus to run. Neither the gazelle nor the lion needs to consciously articulate the reasons it runs. They both act without examining their motivations.

Our customers are running, too. And like the gazelle and the lion, they often don't have the ability or the inclination to explain the underlying motivations that drive their actions. In the first phase of constructing a Brand Model, we delved into the Brand DNA specifically to discover, on a very deep, fundamental level, what underlies our best customers' behaviors.

During this process, we examined the Brand DNA. Identifying the humanistic drivers, archetypal images, cultural stories, and emotional connections that shape our Brand Lovers' relationships with our brand is a critical step, and it serves a critical purpose.

At first glance, that might not be immediately apparent. The Brand DNA tells us a lot about our Brand Lovers. At this point, we know what goes into Brand Lovers, what defines them, and what makes them tick.

It's like having a list of all the ingredients you need to make the world's best brownies. Those brownies need flour, sugar, cocoa, eggs, and nuts. Nike knows what it takes to create its Brand Lovers. It markets itself to customers who identify with the victorious warrior and who enjoy and value feeling confident and strong. Every organization will have its own list of ingredients, its own checklist of essential elements.

Identifying the factors that motivate our best customers—or the ingredients that go into the brownies—gets us started. Now we must embark on the next step in Brand Modeling. It is time to focus on discerning customer insights and identifying meanings.

Customer Insights and the Search for Meaning

We now have to connect the dots, transforming the deep knowledge we've gathered into the framework of the Brand Model. If Brand DNA serves as the foundation that our model is built upon, customer insights and meaning serve as the frame of the building. Customer insights help us to better understand what is important to our customers so that we can serve them better, thereby strengthening the relationship that we have with them.

The accumulation of data in and of itself is not enough to serve our purposes. Consider our ingredients list for brownies once again. Simply buying the flour, eggs, sugar, cocoa powder, and nuts and putting them on the table will not result in a satisfactory experience. You're not getting any brownies that way. There's a process that must be followed, measuring and combining all of the necessary ingredients in a precise and orderly fashion to transform these ingredients into brownies. A mouthful of flour followed by a mouthful of sugar and another of cocoa isn't going to make anyone happy, but when you mix it all up into decadent brownies, it's another story entirely. It all happens when you know the process.

This is the point in Brand Modeling where we focus on process. We know the ingredients that go into creating a Brand Lover. It's time to figure out how they go together. We need an understanding of structure. How are the many disparate elements that make up your Brand DNA manifested in the customer? More important, what does that mean to your organization?

The Reality of Brand Positioning

It is time to revisit a basic truth: branding takes place exclusively in the mind of the customer.

Our brands do not exist outside of the customer's mind. As much as we might like to think we're crafting our brands with clever logo design and amazing taglines, the truth is that our brand positioning comes down to who our best customers believe we are.

To understand what that belief is, and what our brand truly is, we must take the tangled nuances of Brand DNA and view them through a very specific lens. We have to discover what we mean to the customer on a multitude of levels.

Our task is threefold. We have to understand where we fit in the customer's mental landscape, identify why the customer comes to us, and pinpoint with extreme precision the manner in which the customer wants to be engaged.

For all intents and purposes, customer insights are a trifecta of Brand Lover expectations. To be a dominant brand, it's essential not only to understand what those expectations are, but to meet and surpass them consistently. Hit the trifecta and you win big.

This is a critical strength of Brand Modeling. Because Brand Modeling integrates customer insights as a core element, you can gain an element of certainty and confidence in your decision-making process. Every option can be weighed against a clearly defined set of criteria: will this choice fulfill our customer's expectations? If it does, it may be a good decision (other elements in the model will help you determine exactly how good it may be), but if it doesn't, there is no doubt on the table. You are making the wrong choice.

Examining Customer Insights

Customer insights can be divided into three categories. Each category is equally important, and we must understand all three elements completely before we can act upon them in a meaningful fashion. The three categories of customer insight are pillars of belief, tensions, and motivations.

Pillars of belief delineate what our Brand Lovers hold to be true about our organizations. Tensions address the needs that Brand Lovers turn to us to meet. Motivations reveal to us how our best customers want our organization to engage with them.

Pillars of Belief

Positioning happens in the mind of the customer. The pillars of belief articulate the beliefs that our best customers have about our company. This can be a simple but all-important question, such as, "Is it honest and fair? Is it the type of company I want to do business with?" Questions like these can help uncover the beliefs that customers hold about your company that influence their buying decisions.

Brand Lovers strongly prefer to do business with companies that they believe reflect their own personal belief system. They're seeking those points of familiarity, of personal resonance, where their perception of your brand meshes closely with the cultural stories and archetypal images they hold most dear.

Let's say your customers are ardent athletes. They run; they play tennis; they bike. If you asked them about their craziest daydream, you'd hear about competing in the Ironman someday, even though they aren't swimmers! They TiVo the Olympics.

And they need to buy sneakers.

Nike's use of the warrior archetype appeals strongly to these customers. The messages being shared resonate deeply and profoundly. It's easy for a customer to project herself into this ideal, and from here, we see the pillars of belief being formed.

That warrior-athlete needs to succeed. And to succeed, she needs to be prepared. To be prepared, she needs the best gear, and it is her belief that Nike, which is already consistently telling her what she wants to hear, in the way she wants to hear it, provides the best gear.

Perception is reality. Nike sells an awful lot of sneakers. Additionally, the pillars of belief that our warrior-athlete example (and countless others like her) holds so firmly includes the concrete assurance that Nike is the best that she extends that brand loyalty far beyond footwear. Nike loyalists buy Nike apparel, sports equipment, sunglasses, and more. There's even Nike+, which includes a pedometer that works in conjunction with an iPhone app. Strong pillars of belief can hold up a very large roof for your organization to thrive under.

Why Is It Important to Understand Your Brand Lovers' Pillars of Belief?

You may want to ask Blockbuster that question. While it was once the dominant player in the video rental market, an examination of Blockbuster's best customers' pillars of belief might have revealed the following:

- Renting from Blockbuster is expensive.
- It's difficult to find the movies you want at Blockbuster. Popular films are seldom available in a timely fashion—everyone else has already rented them.
- You have to return movies to Blockbuster, and that's a hassle.
- To get a movie from Blockbuster, you must leave your house, then leave it again to return the movie.

Netflix, now the dominant movie rental company, used those pillars of belief to identify viable points of differentiation. It created its organization based around the points where Blockbuster's customers believed the chain was failing. By providing an alternative, it gave customers a chance to form a new series of pillars of belief that were diametrically opposed to what those customers believed about Blockbuster.

It is imperative that you know what your customers believe about your organization. If the pillars of belief you discover include some negatives, this is the two-minute warning. The game's going to be over unless you make some tremendous changes. Belief is a pervasive thing. Once people believe something, it's very difficult to make them change their minds.

Domino's Pizza is engaged in that struggle right now, after very publicly acknowledging that even its Brand Lovers believed its pizza just wasn't very good. Will it be able to turn the tide? Perhaps, but the truly strategic position would have been to stay clued into its Brand Lovers' pillars of belief so that it was never vulnerable to begin with.

How Brand DNA Helps Us Understand Customer Tensions

When we speak about tensions, we're talking about the compelling and complex set of needs that your best customers fulfill by engaging with your company. Tensions can be simultaneously overt (you need something to feed your children for lunch!) and subtle (the expectation that you'll provide your children with the very best of everything despite limited economic resources). Dominant companies consistently succeed by identifying points of unresolved tension and giving the consumer a seamless way to meet all of his needs at the same time.

In other words, that's why choosy moms choose Jif!

Humanistic drivers, archetypal images, cultural stories, and the emotional targets all have a role in crafting what types of tensions our Brand Lovers experience, as well as how they experience those tensions and what they are willing to do in order to have them resolved.

Dominant brands resolve their Brand Lovers' tensions while tapping into and acknowledging the most relevant aspects of their best customers' Brand DNA. Kleenex, a brand so dominant that its name has become synonymous with its category, uses clearly identifiable elements of Brand DNA when marketing its Viva line of paper towels.

The need to nurture and care for others is one of the strongest humanistic drivers. One of the most powerful, universal archetypal images is that of the good mother, omniscient and always caring. Our current cultural mythos certainly involves the story, "Good mothers don't yell at their kids."

A recent Viva campaign shows a small child sharing a playful moment in the kitchen with his mother. Soda gets sprayed everywhere. It's an awful, sticky housekeeping disaster. Yet mom keeps smiling as the announcer shares Viva's tagline: "Life's messy. Clean it up."

This message connects with Viva's Brand Lovers on a number of levels. Homage is paid to the maternal drive, while acknowledging the need to keep one's environment clean and sanitary. The two goals—nurturing and cleaning—could easily be in opposition, but Viva deftly presents a way for its customers to meet their needs. The tension is resolved, and a Brand Lover is born.

Customer Tensions Identify Opportunities

Identifying points of tension in the marketplace inexplicably eludes otherwise savvy business leaders. This is a critical systems failure. If you are listening to your customers, if you are connected to your Brand Lovers, the conversations and engagement that you have with them must include a frank discussion of the problems and challenges they face regularly.

We need look no further than the automobile industry for an example. We've known for almost 40 years that significant changes in gasoline prices can have a dramatic impact on Americans' ability to use their cars in their accustomed fashion. There has been an obvious need for vehicles that run on alternative fuels. Innovators and engineers have responded with a whole suite of solutions. There are cars that run on battery packs and solar cells. Some cars run on ethanol, while others have been retrofitted to use recycled vegetable oil from restaurant deep fryers.

All of these cars would save their owners significant amounts of money on fuel. Yet they haven't really caught on. Why?

It isn't the lingering smell of french fries that emerges from the exhaust of vegetable oil–burning cars that's at fault. (In fact, we understand that to this technology's fanatics, that's a feature, rather than a bug.) Instead, the point of tension lies in the fact that using an alternative-fuel car requires a significant investment by the consumer. And it isn't necessarily a financial investment, either. The problem is that owners of alternative-fuel cars have to invest significant amounts of time, effort, and energy into learning how to fuel their cars. Virtually no infrastructure exists. There are no solar-car garages to perform a tune-up if your car fails to start. Ethanol has been available in gas stations for only a few years now, and it's still not available in every market. No one was really sure how electric cars were supposed to "charge up"—what happens if you get beyond your 30-mile range and run out of juice?

Chevy picked up on this tension. Its latest incarnation of the electric car, the aptly named Volt, resolves the "How do I fuel this thing up?" tension with a simple adapter that can be plugged into any traditional outlet. It's lightweight, portable, and, most of all, easy to understand. You don't need to have an engineering background or understand even basic math to use the Volt. The underlying fear and anxiety that has kept people from exploring alternative-fuel cars has been eliminated with a technology that's easy to understand and use.

The tension—no easy way to fuel alternative vehicles—created an opportunity that Chevy has identified. The Volt was created to resolve the underlying "How am I going to fuel this thing up?" tension.

Identifying and resolving tensions is how dominant organizations win. To identify and resolve tensions, you have to be willing to listen to your best customers. Before you can put their needs first, you need to know what their needs are.

Read the Writing on the Wall

The good thing here, from a leadership perspective, is that this can be easily done. Customers will readily and happily share their tensions with you. Problems and challenges fall easily from their lips. Customers are not shy about sharing what aggravates them. Social media are practically tailor-made for soliciting this information. Tuning out these tales—particularly those that come from Brand Lovers—as nothing more than negativity or criticism is almost a guarantee of disaster.

When there's writing on the wall, you might as well read it. Had Kmart been truly paying attention when Raymond Babbitt (the main character in *Rain Man*) proudly announced, "Kmart sucks!" from the silver screen, it might have done more than file a few poorly advised lawsuits. After that, especially when its disgruntled customer base launched the Kmart Sucks website, the message should have been clear. Kmart's customers were experiencing a lot of tension, and the discount retail chain was doing nothing to resolve it. Kmart's subsequent bankruptcy was among the largest retail bankruptcies ever seen in the United States.

The Ideal Experience: Understanding Customer Motivations

Why does Las Vegas work? It shouldn't. You couldn't pick a worse place to locate a city if you tried. The landscape's brutally harsh. There's not nearly enough water. There's some nifty architecture and big-name entertainment, but other cities have the same things, and it's not nearly so hot there.

It all changes when you drop a dollar in that slot machine and pull the handle. You watch the lights flash, the dials whirl, and suddenly, it happens! You're a winner! The jackpot tumbles out as bells and whistles ring. The take might be only a few hundred dollars—but inside, you feel like a million bucks.

And that—that exhilarating, exceptional, pure feeling of being a winner, of triumphing over the odds and all the ways that Vegas games are purportedly stacked against you, the sensation of being the lucky one—is what keeps Las Vegas alive. That's why people keep coming back. That emotional rush— what we'd call a peak experience—is addictive. Once someone experiences it, he wants it again and again and again. It is hardwired in us. Pleasurable experiences are sought out and repeated.

We can't all be Las Vegas. That's okay, because while the exhilaration that winners experience is an ultimate emotional experience, it's not the only ultimate emotional experience your customers are seeking. Shift the example to a far more down-to-earth business, such as sewer drain cleaning. The emotional connotations of sewer drain cleaning might not leap immediately to mind. However, working with your Brand Lovers to identify the tensions they have—mostly centered on the fact that while it's fine for what happens in Vegas to stay in Vegas, no one wants what happens in the bathroom to stay there indefinitely—leads us to understand the resolution that they're seeking. Vast, overwhelming relief is a peak experience.

Understanding this is central to Brand Model construction.

Where It Counts the Most

- We have to understand the totality of our best customers' expectations: where we fit in these customers' mental landscape, why the customers come to us, and the manner in which the customers want to be engaged.
- The decision-making process becomes simplified. Either a decision is in alignment with our Brand Lovers' expectations or it's not. Decisions that aren't in alignment become obvious nonstarters, saving your organization time, effort, and money.
- Customers strongly prefer to do business with companies that have values and ideals that are in alignment with their own.
- Identifying what negative pillars of belief your Brand Lovers have about your organization provides an opportunity for change and corrective action.
- Understanding the negative pillars of belief that customers have about competing organizations can help you identify profitable opportunities. Netflix did this to Blockbuster.
- Tensions are the signal flags for organizations seeking greater profitability. Where a tension can be identified in the marketplace, an opportunity exists.
- Dominant companies win by identifying and, whenever possible, eliminating points of tension that would keep people from using and enjoying their products.
- Dominant companies win by identifying and delivering the peak emotional experience that their best customers are seeking from them.
- The more pleasurable the peak emotional experience is, the more likely the customer is to repeat it.

CHAPTER 8

Setting Your Brand Apart from the Competition

Everybody has to eat. There's no way around it. Feeding yourself regularly is a requirement. We're on the ground level of Maslow's hierarchy here: if you fail to ingest food on a regular basis, your health will deteriorate rapidly. We could live our lives eating nothing but egg white omelets and whole wheat toast, but most people crave a little more variety. By and large, we select food that we find attractive and that tastes good.

The question then becomes, where do you go for your groceries? The answer to that question has to do with convenience and price. It also has to do with the shopper's self-image. To examine what separates the Whole Foods shopper from the Safeway shopper, we can move on to the next stage in Brand Modeling: discerning points of differentiation through your brand's identity.

You Say Tomato, I Say Organic Heirloom Cherokee Purple Bliss

For a long time, the biggest problem a tomato farmer had was, "How do I grow a tomato that's tough enough to stand up to being shipped thousands of miles in less than ideal conditions and arrive attractive enough to appeal to a produce buyer who has no other choices?" The actual flavor of the tomato in question was a secondary, sometimes tertiary, concern. The consumer who wanted to buy a "fresh" tomato either took what you shipped to the store or went without.

It was a system that was destined to fail. Consumers had an alternative, albeit either a labor-intensive one or an expensive one. People who wanted flavorful tomatoes knew that they had to either grow them themselves or pay top dollar for hothouse tomatoes (which were not often available but always expensive).

The marketplace took notice. Farmers' markets and the fledgling local foods movement introduced heirloom tomatoes—full of flavor, but a shipper's nightmare—to the buying public. At first, the phenomenon was covered only by the food industry press, but it soon spilled over into consumer magazines. Suddenly, the *Redbook* reader was confronted with tips about "new" tomato varieties that looked terrible but tasted fabulous.

Not every reader was motivated to buy those heirloom tomatoes, but some were. Identifying who those shoppers were became a critical task, not only for tomato farmers, but for grocery chain owners identifying their points of differentiation.

Taste is not the only reason that people select heirloom tomatoes. There are many complex psychosocial reasons that jump right into the grocery basket along with each lumpy, bumpy, fragile Cherokee Purple or Pink Lady.

Some shoppers opt for heirloom varieties for the snob appeal. If the foodie magazines and TV chefs are touting heirloom tomatoes as the best, then they want the best for their family, because they are the type of people who provide the best. Others may select heirloom varieties out of a sense of nostalgia, trying to connect with flavors that remind them of their mothers, or their grandmothers, or ancestors that they never really got a chance to know at all. Still other heirloom aficionados will tell you about preserving a culinary heritage, supporting small farmers, moving toward a more natural way of eating, simplifying life, and so on.

It's just as important to know who doesn't buy or know about heirloom tomatoes. There are customers who may very much want to be able to buy heirloom tomatoes, but lack the funds to do so. There are customers who wouldn't buy a fresh vegetable on a bet, heirloom or otherwise. There are customers who find the very concept of heirloom tomatoes an elaborate demonstration of an elitist culture gone awry, an affectation that they protest by buying all of their tomatoes in ketchup form.

If you're a grocery chain owner, you'd better know your Brand Lovers' position on tomatoes. Understanding your Brand Lovers' feelings on the heirloom tomato issue—and, more critically, why they feel the way they do—can help you pinpoint the best way to differentiate your business from all of your competitors.

Why Do They Want You? What Brand Lovers Love Most

Every business has its Brand Lovers. What we need to examine at this point is why your Brand Lovers love you. What is it about your organization that motivates customers to shop with you time and time again?

Examining our Brand Lovers' Brand DNA allowed us to develop customer insights—a deep and concrete understanding of what's important to our Brand Lovers. Now we have to identify those points of alignment where the unique characteristics and features of our business trigger strong, positive, actionable emotional responses in our Brand Lovers.

To bring this back to our tomato question, for example, as the owner of a grocery chain, it would help tremendously to know how the store's Brand Lovers feel about issues of sustainability and local produce. If these are issues that the Brand Lovers feel passionately about, then opting to offer heirloom tomatoes and promote them heavily makes good business sense. You're offering your customers more, on an emotional level, of what they've already demonstrated they've found important. This is a valuable point of differentiation. You're giving your customers a reason to buy from you.

When Whole Foods shoppers, for example, encounter a new variety of heirloom tomatoes attractively presented on the shelves, they're pleased, because this is a product that they will find awesome in an environment in which they expect this kind of awesomeness.

The tomatoes are not, in and of themselves, any more or less awesome when they wind up on the shelves at Safeway. However, the likelihood that Safeway shoppers will have a strong positive emotional reaction to the introduction of heirloom tomatoes is not nearly as great. Why? It comes back to examining why Safeway shoppers love Safeway. Price and a perception of value are strong drivers for Safeway shoppers. They are not likely to see the introduction of a relatively high-priced produce item as being in alignment with their expectations of the store. It doesn't fit. While the presence of heirloom tomatoes may not hurt the relationship that Safeway enjoys with its Brand Lovers, it's not doing anything to strengthen that connection.

Additionally, you have to consider the opportunity cost that Safeway incurs when it chooses to stock heirloom tomatoes. Choosing to feature something that isn't of interest or value to your best customers uses time, effort, and resources that could be better devoted to featuring something that is relevant and of interest to them. You're losing a valuable opportunity to be of service to your customers. Each of these opportunities comes only once. When it's gone, it's gone.

Differentiation begins by identifying what your Brand Lovers love most about doing business with you and providing more of that. Differentiation ends—or takes on a new dimension—when it is done so completely and so well that your organization achieves a dominant position in the industry and your competition is rendered irrelevant.

We Don't Sell Cheetos Here: What Whole Foods Teaches Us About Brand Positioning

You can buy many things at Whole Foods. There's wild-caught salmon that melts in your mouth. There are eggs from chickens that have never seen the inside of a cage. There's cheese from every corner of the world. You can get Greek feta and French chèvre and Parmigiano Reggiano fresh from the Italian countryside.

What you cannot get, however, is Cheetos. Walk every aisle, scour every shelf, look into every nook and cranny, and nowhere will you find the telltale neon orange, puffed crunchiness of Cheetos. Ask a Whole Foods employee where you might find some Cheetos, and he'll direct you to another store. (Unless, of course, he's fainted from shock. Ask these questions carefully, if you must ask them.)

Whole Foods has built its brand around its core values, which include a commitment to selling pure, natural food. On its website, it says, "When you shop with us, you won't find artificial flavors, colors, sweeteners, preservatives or those nasty trans fats. We just offer real food, pure and simple."

Almost every other major grocery chain in America sells Cheetos.

If you want to render your organization's competition irrelevant, you first have to know what your competition is doing. Whole Foods touts, "It's good to be different," but you can be different only if you know what you're differing yourself from.

This is about far more than merchandise selection. It's not enough to not sell Cheetos. You have to know why your customers wouldn't want them.

Brand positioning means examining every aspect of your organization's operation and presentation and comparing it with how your competition does business. While products and service offerings are an obvious and immediate way to differentiate your organization, they're no longer enough. A superb shopping experience can make or break a company.

Bear in mind, too, that it's imperative that you have a very broad definition of "competition." Whole Foods certainly competes with the Safeways, Wegmans, and Hannafords of the world, but it's also up against restaurants, farmers' markets, and mom's standing invitation to bring everyone over for dinner. Your Brand Lover has options both within and outside your industry. It is essential that you examine where your organization is positioned in relation to all of them.

Being different isn't the same as differentiation. Kroger's is different from Safeway, yet customers can and do shop at the two interchangeably. To achieve the dominant position that Whole Foods enjoys within its market, your organization must be significantly different in ways that your Brand Lovers find particularly meaningful.

Understanding meaningful differences becomes possible only when we understand completely and fully how our customers see us. To do this, we have to examine the Brand Ecosystem.

Whole Foods in the Wild: The Brand Ecosystem

If we want to know why Whole Foods is so successful and how this chain became the dominant player in the natural foods grocery sector, we have to understand the natural foods grocery sector as a whole. Context matters. We can examine Whole Foods all day long, but without a fundamental understanding of the environment that Whole Foods operates in, we're missing a huge part of the picture.

Nothing exists in isolation. Every organization, in every industry, belongs to a number of communities, all composed of colleagues and competitors. Harley-Davidson, for example, is part of a huge community as a motorcycle manufacturer. It shares space with Yamaha, Honda, Kawasaki, Orange County Choppers, BMW, and more. When we look at Harley-Davidson as a lifestyle brand, another community reveals itself. From this perspective, we see Harley-Davidson keeping company with Volkswagen, MINI Cooper, BMW, and even Porsche. All of these brands have freedom and an exceptional driving experience at the heart of their Brand Ecosystem. You can see that there are some brands that appear in both groups. When we take up all of the communities that a brand belongs to, and combine them, we have the Brand Ecosystem: a comprehensive examination of the space the brand occupies in the consumer's mind.

Why Is the Brand Ecosystem Important?

When we're examining the Brand Ecosystem, we're trying to discern two things. The first thing we need to discover is the exact place the organization currently occupies in the marketplace.

Not all brands are created equal, and no one is more aware of this fact than the consumer. The people who are responsible for creating brands are also intimately involved in imposing hierarchies and rankings upon them. One organization generally occupies a dominant position, with every other company in that sector positioning itself in relation to that leader. Apple rose from the ashes to become an envied competitor and went on to redefine the computer market according to its own vision, a market that includes tablets as a viable personal computing option. Other computer companies, like HP, have accepted this new definition, and now are in the unenviable position of vying to stake out the most profitable share of what remains in the marketplace. How do Hewlett-Packard, Dell, and Gateway compare to Apple, and to each other?

Examining market share numbers gives us some of the answer, but perhaps not the most important part. Analyzing customers' perception of the market as a whole, and the various brands within it, from a number of perspectives gives us a more complete understanding. It becomes possible to understand not only the relative size of the organizations in question, but what role they play in the consumer's mind.

It's Good to Be the Lead Sled Dog

Where does your company exist within the Brand Ecosystem? When biologists talk about an ecosystem, they assign each animal and plant within it a role. You've heard of alpha predators: the sharks, wolves, and bears that occupy the top of the food chain. Other life forms have a place as well. Some are strictly food. Some are both predator and prey.

When we're talking about organizations, things become a little bit more complex. Generally, it's fairly easy to identify the dominant organization within an industry. When a company is far and away the leader, there's no question about who's on top. No other watch is a Rolex. But how do you classify the other companies in the sector? Citizen, Hermès, Movado, and Breitling all have their places in the luxury watch market. The trick is determining exactly what that place is.

Understanding the Brand Ecosystem is critical for organizations that wish to achieve a dominant place in the market. When you are a dominant organization, there are no easy substitutes in the customer's mind. A Harley owner won't be happy with a Kawasaki motorcycle. Apple aficionados have been known to claim physical pain from being forced to use a PC.

If you're not a dominant organization yet, the consumer has an easier time finding alternative sources for your products and services. A love for Häagen-Dazs's ice cream seldom precludes anyone from enjoying Breyers. The points of differentiation between companies are not necessarily as meaningful to the customer. Convenience and price take on larger roles in driving customer behavior.

If your company isn't already in a dominant position, understanding the brand ecosystem can help your organization define those areas where it can form stronger, more meaningful psychological and emotional bonds with its best customers. This can help move your company closer to the dominant position in the marketplace. Rolex may define the luxury watch for the general public, but Breitling has carved out its own high-end niche by focusing on adventurers. Appealing to pilots and other professionals who value extreme precision in a timepiece and embodying a message of skilled macho competence have given the company a place where it's no longer chasing Rolex. It's profitable and dominant within its niche.

It may be that an organization doesn't yet have a well-defined place in the Brand Ecosystem. New organizations can use their understanding of the Brand Ecosystem to pinpoint the place they'd like to occupy within it. Coupling this direction with the understanding that Brand Modeling provides is the most efficient way to help a company gain its desired place in the market.

Food for Thought: Whole Foods and the Brand Ecosystem

When we look at Whole Foods, we also have to look at other natural foods grocery stores, and also at other types of grocery stores. Whole Foods shares the natural foods community with Trader Joe's, Earth Fare, The Fresh Market, and dozens of smaller, regional chains.

When we consider Whole Foods as a national grocery chain, we find that there are numerous companies in the community like Aldi's, Costco, the Delhaize group (Food Lion, Hannaford, and more), Kroger, Piggly Wiggly, Safeway, Super Value (Save-A-Lot, Shop 'n Save), SuperTarget, and Walmart Supercenters. There are also hundreds of regional and local grocery stores, all of which play a role in defining Whole Foods' place in the market.

Whole Foods has occupied numerous places within these communities. More than 30 years ago, the company had a single store in Austin, Texas. At that time, the entire natural foods grocery store community was relatively small and scattered. A few stores had achieved small chain status, but the vast majority of natural food stores were single-location independent operations.

Whole Foods' vision—a large part of the reason it's so appealing to its Brand Lovers—has always included an expansive approach. The tagline "Whole Foods, Whole People, Whole Planet" speaks to a drive that wouldn't be filled with a single location. This required Whole Foods to have a comprehensive, in-depth understanding of all the other grocery stores that its customers were currently shopping at and what it would take to convert those customers into Whole Foods shoppers.

This type of in-depth analysis isn't easy, and it requires a substantial investment of energy and resources. However, having a concrete understanding of the Brand Ecosystem provides a competitive advantage that is nearly impossible for others to beat. Whole Foods was able to learn from and emulate what other grocery chains were doing well (product placement and displays), identify and overtake the competition in areas where those chains were weak (organic and natural options), and, most important of all, pinpoint those emotional and psychological points where the chain could differentiate itself from every other competitor, thereby securing its dominant place in the market.

Building Brand Identity

The term *Brand Identity* is something you've heard before. Lots of times, we hear it used to describe the visual aspects of branding: color choices and logo design, the images used in advertisements and on websites. But this is a really incomplete definition of identity. Defining Brand Identity this way is tantamount to describing yourself by listing the contents of your wardrobe. Do the clothes you wear completely describe who you are as a person?

We must go deeper. The visual elements are important, of course, but what we're after is a comprehensive understanding of who the brand is in the eyes of its best customers.

Your Brand Identity is the totality of how your best customers view their direct engagement with your brand. That's a really complicated way to say, "How do your Brand Lovers see you?"

Baby, You've Got Personality

It's very common to hear Brand Lovers describing organizations in terms we'd normally hear being used to describe a best friend. An organization might be referred to as quirky or fun or energetic or trustworthy.

What's happening here is the pervasive human tendency toward personification. We love to attribute human characteristics to something that isn't human at all. That's why you'll hear about a charming café or a stubborn software problem.

Organizations are made up of people, so the tendency to personify them is strong. Dominant organizations go with this innate tendency and make the personification a key part of their Brand Identity. Articulating that personification is what's known as a personality analogue. What type of person would your organization be, if it were a person? Steve Jobs, for example, personifies the Apple brand.

One of the best examples of this concept in action turns out to not be a person at all. Geico's lizard—charming, self-depreciating, friendly, and frank about both the customer's expectations of service and her desire for low prices—resonates powerfully and effectively with Geico's Brand Lovers.

Brand Identity from Every Angle

Brand Identity is not strictly a visual phenomenon, as we are not strictly visual creatures. Admittedly, we process a disproportionate amount of information visually, but that's only the beginning of the story. It's important to consider all of the senses when crafting a Brand Identity, as well as factoring in what we know about emotional intelligence to forge connections on a less tangible level.

Let's start with the visuals and move on from there. Imagery is perhaps the most accessible portion of Brand Identity. Here we're talking about the images and symbols that your Brand Lovers associate with your organization. What makes your organization "look" like you?

Ideally, customers should be able to tell at a glance not only who you are, but what type of business you're in and how you conduct yourself while you're doing it. Much of the information our customers take in comes strictly from visual cues. We're telling our customers what type of experience they can expect by the way we use imagery. If we're smart and strategic, we're selecting the images that have the most appeal and emotional resonance for our Brand Lovers.

Dominant brands are particularly effective at using symbols and iconography to connect with their Brand Lovers. Examples are everywhere, from the Nike swoosh to the Marlboro man and Harley-Davidson's shield and eagle wings. These symbols are rooted in a deep archetypal understanding that has been proven to resonate with the brand's best customers. In a way, they serve as a sort of visual shorthand, letting the viewer understand a great deal of information in a limited time frame.

But that's not all. Moving beyond iconography, your brand imagery extends to include other visual cues that your Brand Lovers associate with your brand.

Apple Stores are visually stunning, wide-open spaces, full of white and primary colors. Harley-Davidson's "look" is black leather with orange accents, fringe and chrome and big bearded men riding motorcycles on the open road. Whole Foods stocks its shelves to create the image of abundance. Those towering pyramids of pristine apples, pears, and pineapples didn't appear by accident.

You Can Hear or You Can Listen

Our first experience of the world comes through our ears. Long before we're born, we hear our mother's heartbeat, comforting and secure. In the early days of infancy, when we cannot see more than a few feet in front of us with any clarity, we can discern subtle differences in sound. We know our mother's voice and our father's voice, the sounds that delight us and shape our view of who we are.

Even after we're grown, auditory cues still play a huge role in how we process information. Sound will get a response out of us more quickly than anything else. Emergency sirens are set at a specific pitch and volume because that makes them impossible to ignore.

We also tend to remember sounds, particularly distinctive sounds, and form associative memories with them. The thudding rumble of a Harley's exhaust is recognizable to any Brand Lover. Harley knows how valuable this is. It even tried to patent the sound, abandoning the effort only after years of fruitless litigation. Other examples include the hiss of the espresso machine and the clatter of beverage preparation at Starbucks. These sounds are as much a part of your Brand Identity as the sign out front or the uniforms you have your people wear. They are sounds that define you in the mind of the Brand Lover.

Pinpointing what sounds your Brand Lovers associate with your organization can also provide greater insight into why they love your organization. This is the difference between listening and hearing. The loud Harley rumble is distinctive and cool, but why is it cool? Only by talking with your Brand Lovers can you tap into the deeper meaning that particular sound has for them. It may be the sense of being an outsider, a free spirit, one who doesn't necessarily have to play nicely and by the rules, someone who's not afraid to be larger than life and live out loud—an awful lot of meaning can be hidden in the roar of chromed pipes.

More than a Feeling

Our skin is our largest sensory organ. We're built to process the world through touch, but a complex tangle of social norms and cultural dysfunctions has transformed us to such an extent that many people forget that they have a sense of touch.

Yet tactile experiences—the sensations we feel, including temperature, texture, pressure, and proximity—are hugely important. An essential part of building Brand Identity is identifying and articulating your brand's kinesthetic components. This means capturing the primary and core tactile feelings associated with your brand.

Part of Whole Foods' identity can be linked directly to its understanding of its brand kinesthetics. Customers are encouraged to touch its produce, to feel the apples and heft the cantaloupe and get a good sense of what a delicious dinner feels like ahead of time.

Coach mirrors much of the spatial experience of being in an art gallery or a museum in its retail space. Wide-open spaces, a sense of being alone with the object you're viewing, and an almost puritanical eschewing of everything that detracts from the art all contribute to the "feel" that you're in the presence of something noteworthy and remarkable. In this case, that remarkable presence is the Coach bag.

All five senses can be used to cement a Brand Lover's connection to the organization. Coach bags certainly have a scent of their own. The aroma of luxury and leather is one that its Brand Lovers cannot resist. Singapore Airlines, which is slowly but steadily carving out its own distinct market share, uses a distinctive fragrance in its planes to help further differentiate the flying experience.

Crafting Your Messaging Strategy

Bringing together the points of differentiation that are most valued by your Brand Lovers with a concrete understanding of how your brand is experienced and shared by your best customers brings you to the point where you can develop a messaging strategy.

The reason that messaging strategies developed through the Brand Modeling process are particularly effective is that you now have a vehicle that delivers what the brand is saying in the way in which the customer is predisposed to hear it. This strengthens and reinforces your relationship with your Brand Lovers, as well as making your organization more appealing to Brand Lovers you haven't met yet.

Where It Counts the Most

- Identify those critical points of alignment where your bond with your Brand Lovers is the strongest. These are your points of differentiation. Emphasize them and win.
- The humanistic drivers that lead your Brand Lovers to choose you over any other competitor come into play at every point in your operation. From the merchandise you choose to the people you hire to the messaging you use, every point of contact must honor those humanistic drivers.
- You can differentiate your brand effectively only if you know what you're trying to differentiate yourself from. Dominant organizations have a complete understanding of the Brand Ecosystem—the market environment that their company operates in.
- Customers always have options, both within your industry and outside of it. It's important to know who are all the competitors for your Brand Lovers' attention and affection.
- Communities can be defined in a number of ways, including tangible criteria, such as type of product and service, or intangible criteria, such as common humanistic drivers.
- Let other people make mistakes for you. Identify areas where your competitors are weak, and avoid the missteps that made these companies vulnerable.
- Your brand already has a personality in the customer's mind. Your job is to find out what your Brand Lovers think that personality is.
- Dominant organizations win by identifying and harnessing universally appealing iconography, then packaging that iconography in a way that their Brand Lovers will find appealing to continually reinforce their messaging.

- Dominant organizations win by creating environments that cater to all of their Brand Lovers' senses. They find the best way to be visually appealing, pinpoint distinctive sounds, and create a tactile environment that resonates.

CHAPTER 9

Your Brand's Vision

You've flown into a strange city for a conference. It's quite a distance from the airport to your destination, the Palm Woods Center, but you're not sweating it. You've got a rental car and a GPS. What could possibly go wrong? All you have to do is punch in the name of the conference center and the adventure begins.

At first, everything seems fine. The GPS guides you from the rental counter through the unfamiliar streets. As the turn-by-turn directions take you farther and farther from the airport, however, you begin to suspect that something's wrong. You're headed to a conference, but the directions you've been given are leading you into an industrial area, and then a postindustrial area with shuttered factory windows and empty parking lots. From there, you drive into what appears to be a postapocalyptic area, where every building sports a broken window or two and glass graces the gutter, promising to chew through your tires if you stray too close to the curb. The people watching your slow, wary progress down the street don't look all that thrilled to see you, but the GPS promises that your destination is 0.2 mile ahead.

In 0.2 mile, you find yourself looking at the Palm Woods, but it's not the upscale conference center you were expecting. Instead, you're looking at a burned-out nightclub that's clearly been out of business for quite a while.

One frantic phone call later and you're on your way to the conference center—learning only now that if you want the GPS to guide you to the Palm Woods, you have to ask for it by its old name, Cedar Point. The GPS maps haven't been updated since new owners took over. Chalk one up to map failure.

As business leaders, we're facing the exact same challenge that those GPS programmers are struggling with. Conditions are changing all the time. We operate in a dynamic environment. The highways to success that served previous generations reliably may now be rutted, decrepit roads to ruin.

We need more information than the GPS can provide. Before we start driving, we need reports on road conditions and insight concerning what kind of journey to expect. Simply having the name isn't enough. We knew we were headed to Palm Woods, after all, and look what good that did us!

In much the same way, if we're trying to move our organization to a more profitable, dominant position in the marketplace, we need to know where that place is and what it looks like. It would help tremendously to have a complete and detailed map.

Unfortunately, there's no mapmaker waiting in the wings to draw this map for us. We need to be our own cartographers, charting our route to greatness ourselves. Because we have not yet arrived, we're creating a map that is in many ways speculative. Brand Modeling allows us to ramp up the accuracy and reliability of this map by pooling several sources of information about our destination, a process that we call creating a Brand Vision. A Brand Vision allows us to identify the tools we need to move our organization effectively and efficiently into alignment with our Brand Lovers—the point of ultimate profitability.

The Role of Brand Vision

What does success look like for your organization? Every company has its own definition. Brand Vision reveals all the components of organizational triumph: who your best customers are, what your organization represents in the marketplace, how the company functions, and what, ultimately, motivates customers to do business with you.

Dominant organizations put significant emphasis on crafting a complete, comprehensive Brand Vision. The more fully realized and detailed this conceptualization is, the more effective it becomes as a decision-making and forecasting tool.

Your Brand Vision articulates your brand's ideals. It introduces a significant measure of efficiency into the organizational decision-making process. If you know that one decision will move you closer to your brand's essence and another will move you further away from it, making the right choice becomes a no-brainer. You can avoid wasted steps, effort, and expense. Every decision, potential campaign, or proposed new direction is weighed against a single criterion: will this get us to where we want to be? The question can be refined endlessly. Will pursuing this option allow us to become successful in the most effective fashion? Are we being efficient? This unity of vision affords significant advantages, as it provides a blueprint for ongoing success, securing and keeping a dominant position in the marketplace. It is a tool that smart leaders use to win the war before the battle even starts.

Brand Vision is the single most important tool that marketing leaders have.

Components of Brand Vision

Being a leader is rooted in the ability to conceptualize where you want your organization to go, and the skill set to reasonably project what it is going to take to get there. This conceptualization can be powerful, strong, and compelling.

Unfortunately, it's not enough in and of itself. For one thing, it's not complete, and there's really no way to be sure it's accurate.

Consumer behavior and market trends exist as dynamic states. They're never static. How consumers feel and act evolves in response to changing conditions. The customers we have today are not the same customers we had before the recession started. They've been changed deeply and profoundly by economic circumstances. That's only one example. Every factor that affects our customers' lives can alter their relationships with us.

It doesn't matter how long you've been in business. There is no level of experience that will allow you to foresee every reaction your customer base will have to life's events. There are no absolutes guaranteed to be found in examining human behavior, only discovery.

Yet, proficient leaders can predict, with a reasonably high degree of certainty, what they're likely to discover. This is more than an educated guess. It is the cumulative effect of highly focused experience, research, and preparation. Leveraging knowledge, data, insight, and skill makes it possible to achieve the dominant position in even the most competitive marketplace. Surprises remain, however, and that's where your Brand Lovers enter the picture.

Brand Lovers and Brand Vision: Where They Connect

Our Brand Lovers have a critical role. Not only are they the part of our customer base that is the most loyal, profitable, and enthusiastic, but Brand Lovers guide our organization to the place in the market where we can be most successful. By following them, we will reach the point where we can enjoy ultimate profitability and brand dominance. There's just one question: how do Brand Lovers do that?

Brand Lovers are drawn to other Brand Lovers and to people who have the potential to be Brand Lovers. In other words, our best customers look for individuals whom they perceive as being like them. There are critical traits that are essential to a Brand Lover's identity. Brand Lovers gravitate, unfailingly, to others who share those same essential traits. This is as certain as the sun rising in the east. The pattern never changes.

To start filling in our map and clarifying our Brand Vision, we need to know what makes one Brand Lover recognize another. What are those essential characteristics that are so strong and compelling that they lead a Brand Lover to choose this brand rather than another?

What we're looking for is the defining qualities of our Brand Lovers, reduced to a tight, taut description. We need the essential information and no more. What are the three or four clues we can use to say, "These people are like our best customers." And, more important, "These people have the potential to become our Brand Lovers."

This Brand Lover identification articulates how your best customers see themselves. How would your most profitable, loyal, vocal customers describe themselves?

The answers to this question serve as guidepost markers along the trail. As your organization moves more and more into alignment with your Brand Lovers, the numbers of your most loyal, most profitable customers should increase. A consistent pattern of customer types will emerge, defined by the three or four key traits your Brand Lovers have defined as accurate descriptors of themselves. If you're not seeing Brand Lovers, or if their numbers drop off significantly, you know you're headed in the wrong direction.

To determine three key traits that define your Brand Lovers requires leveraging analytical and psychological techniques. Some of our best customers are shy, or not terribly self-aware. They're focused on living lives that give them joy and happiness, not on what makes your brand more profitable. Using metaphorical models, such as asking what type of person your brand would be if it came to life, can yield more useful results than asking for three descriptive phrases. These terms are often idealized. Brand Lovers tend to see themselves in the best possible light. They will describe themselves both as they actually are and as they'd like to be.

At this point, it's a matter of combining the sets of data and analyzing them critically. Getting to our desired result—three or four adjectives that describe the Brand Lover with pinpoint accuracy—can be an art form in itself. By sifting through the accumulated statements for similar phrases and frequently appearing words, you can begin to rough out a selection. From there, it's time to move on to testing those phrases to see which of them resonate most strongly with your best customers.

When you determine the definitive three or four adjectives, which we'll be calling Brand Lover characteristics, you have a critical tool to help your organization reach its goals. Every action that the organization takes, both behind the scenes and at every point of customer contact, must make your Brand Lovers feel as if they're at home, in the company of other people who think and act the way they do. Your Brand Lovers provide direction and guidance, which are critical to operating in the most efficient, effective manner.

HBO and Brand Lover Characteristics

HBO is the undisputed king of the premium cable content market. More than 28 million people subscribe to HBO, and countless more catch HBO programming such as *The Sopranos*, *Sex and the City*, and *Deadwood* as it is reaired on other networks. HBO has proven that there's an audience for edgy, intelligent television—original programming that might not be allowed on other stations.

This audience, HBO's Brand Lovers, responded by becoming avid viewers of HBO content. Their enthusiastic support of HBO programming propelled the network into a dominant position. When HBO has a concrete understanding of who its Brand Lovers are, it becomes easier for it to produce new shows that will appeal to existing viewers, attract new eyes to the station, and further cement the brand's reputation for excellence.

To begin, let's look at HBO's Brand Lovers. How do the people who are so passionate about HBO programming look when the camera's turned on them? How do HBO's Brand Lovers see themselves? What is it about watching HBO that is so important to them?

The answers we get to those questions might look something like this: HBO viewers pride themselves on their intelligence and their expansive worldview. They value captivating storytelling. They want to be engrossed—but that's not all. HBO viewers want to be challenged. They like programming that confronts societal norms and pushes the envelope. They enjoy discovering new worldviews.

HBO programming does contain more explicit sex, violence, and profanity than can be found on any other network's shows. This is part of the brand's cachet. This is a space where the boundaries are fluid, and anything could happen. There is an implicit contract that is central to the HBO experience: in exchange for cutting-edge dramatic content, viewers agree to leave their traditional mores and mindset at the door. Here, it is understood, you might be offended, but it will be totally worth it.

Reducing that to a series of descriptive adjectives requires insight, analysis, and some judgment calls. If we were to offer some terms for HBO's list, we would want to suggest terms like *radically intelligent*, *postconventional*, and *bold explorers*.

Your Team and Your Brand Vision

It takes more than direction to bring your company to the highest levels of performance. It's great to know where you're going, but it's better to have the endurance, skills, and resources to get there. Your key managers and the employees you depend on provide the attributes you need to turn the plan into reality. Without their input, it would be impossible to tell what's going to motivate your team members to keep performing at the highest level, even when conditions get tough.

Your team members provide valuable insight into how you're going to reach your goals. What's your company's working style? How does your team operate? Every organization faces the challenges of business in a unique way. You need to know clearly and concretely what your team's approach is and how to make it work effectively. Dominant organizations examine and understand the team's expectations and make a point of meeting and even surpassing those expectations.

How Do You Make It to the Top?

How is your team going to ascend to the top spot in the market? Every organization has a unique set of core strengths and talents. What we need is more than an organizational résumé. We're looking for an articulation of not only what your company can do, but how you do it.

Another way to look at this question is from the Brand Lovers' perspective. Just as we outlined how our best customers look for people who resemble themselves, our Brand Lovers have certain expectations of how our organization will act.

What would your Brand Lovers say your organization stands for? If they had to predict how you would act when there was a problem with your products and services, what would those predictions look like? In short, what type of organization are you?

How we conduct ourselves plays a large role in our customers' relationship with us. An organization can attract Brand Lovers with values that are rooted in the company's identity—Apple's innovation, for example, or Harley's embrace of the open road—or with evidentiary values, which are articulated in the way a company conducts itself. Prior to 1995, Ben & Jerry's, the eco-friendly ice cream darlings from Vermont, built tremendous brand equity with its policy that the highest-paid employee would make no more than five times what the lowest-paid employee was paid.

This is the point in the mapmaking process where the diagnostic qualities of Brand Modeling take center stage. It is entirely possible for a business's leadership to be fundamentally disconnected from what its Brand Lovers are saying, which makes it incredibly difficult for the business to be successful. If there's a significant disconnect between how Brand Lovers see an organization and how that organization sees itself, it will manifest during this discussion.

How we operate our business affects our customers' experience of our organization. If you wish to be perceived as trustworthy, for example, the everyday performance of your organization must be dependable and delivered with integrity.

What Motivates Your Team?

The second question to consider, from the team's point of view, is one of motivation. Why are we all joining together in this endeavor? What is our common cause, and what drives each individual member of the organization to be a part of it? Every person who joins your organization, from C-level executives to frontline staff, has his own reasons for signing up. It's critical to know what it takes to keep your team members excited, enthused, and engaged.

In order to reach the best position in the marketplace, an organization absolutely needs a dependable team that works well together toward a common goal. This doesn't happen automatically. Effective leaders put significant amounts of time and effort into constructing and maintaining well-balanced, effective teams.

This level of cohesion and unity of purpose is equally critical for organizations that are determined to reach the top. Unless the entirety of your organization is working to reach the same goal, you'll never get there. If some team members have different goals and are determined to pursue a different agenda, you'll have a problem. If some team members are fine with the plan, but they don't want to do the work the plan requires, you'll have a problem. Organizational success is dependent upon the unity of vision and purpose of all of the participants. In other words, you need a strong, healthy corporate culture.

How is the organization seen by its employees? A company's corporate culture can be seen as the overt recognition of the relationship between the organization and its employees, as well as an ongoing discussion and assessment of the relationship, what motivates both parties, and how well it's working for everyone involved. Every member of the team needs to understand what is expected of her. Every member of the team needs to be recognized for her contributions and feel invested in making sure the organization is successful.

These cultural values are already present in your organization. These are the tenets your organization is using each and every day as you move closer to your goals. Decisions have been made, priorities recognized, and actions taken that have gotten your company where it is today. Your team has already told you what's important to it. The information may not be idealized or well articulated, but it's there. Employees and stakeholders alike have a sense of what an organization stands for and what is the most critical motivating force guiding corporate decision.

To make this understanding a valuable component of your map, you need an overt, organized articulation of your organization's driving values. Then you need to ensure that these values are understood and embraced by everyone within your organization. When these values permeate the entire culture, you will have happier and more productive employees who will ultimately serve your customers the way you serve your employees. In other words, the team will make faster progress when it believes that the company will be successful and that playing a role in achieving organizational success will yield specific meaningful and personal rewards. This is the team members' own Brand Vision.

Integrating the why component into your Brand Vision plays a pivotal role in attracting and retaining high-value employees, but that's only part of the picture. Equally critical is its role as a known parameter in decision making. Is a proposed action directly in alignment with your culture's values or not?

Google cites its "Don't be evil" mantra as a critical component in identifying which opportunities are viable options. What makes a decision evil? To answer that question, you have to understand a particularly nuanced aspect of corporate culture: the company's perception of itself.

Getting to the Top and Staying There: Why Google Wins

Google, with its ubiquitous presence and unquestioned dominance in the search arena, depends upon its team members to create and innovate. This dependency makes it critical for Google to have a strong, supportive corporate culture. Team cohesion is at a premium.

Over the years, Google has released versions of "Ten Things We Know to Be True." It begins with "Focus on the user and all else will follow" and concludes with "Great just isn't good enough." In between come the guiding principles that the company has followed during its rise to the top:

- It's best to do one thing really, really well.
- Fast is better than slow.
- Democracy on the web works.
- You don't need to be at your desk to need an answer.
- You can make money without doing evil.
- There's always more information out there.
- The need for information crosses all borders.
- You can be serious without needing a suit.

Each statement tells us something important about Google. It's important to note that what Google does—and what other dominant organizations do—is consciously create and articulate a core set of values that the company lives by. These are not theoretical statements that get handed to every new employee as part of his orientation. They are living, breathing values that play a critical role in the everyday operation of the organization. This is how it reaches the top, detailed step by step.

Google lives by these statements. Its focus on search is intense and complete. Visit the Google home page and you find, beneath the sometimes-quirky Google logo, a simple search box. That's it. Nothing else. Search is what Google is all about. It is best to do one thing really, really well.

Visit the home page of one of Google's leading competitors, Yahoo!. Here the picture is different. You'll find a search box, but that's not all. There are top entertainment headlines, trending topics, advertising, must-see video, and a poll where you can share your opinion on the most pressing question of the day. There's no sense of clarity or focus. If Yahoo! is doing one thing very well, no one's really sure what that one thing is.

"Great just isn't good enough" sounds great. Putting those words into action so that they produce results will look different for every organization. For Google, it's meant offering its engineers "20 percent time," time that can be used to pursue individual projects and passions. This is a significant commitment—we're talking about a full day every week for every single engineer—but it's yielded significant results for Google. The company reports that Google Suggest, Adsense for Content, and Orkut have all come out of 20 percent time.

More important, 20 percent time is Google's acknowledgment that the creative process requires time and freedom. It understands what motivates its employees. What better incentive can there be for a creative, innovative individual than the resources, freedom, and encouragement to find answers to questions, try new solutions, and create tomorrow's information paradigm?

Google's approach is strong because it recognizes the difficulties inherent in mountain climbing. There is an overt understanding that there are no perfect days, that innovation takes time, and that promising ideas sometimes lead absolutely nowhere. Even so, the message remains clear: innovation is job one, as long as that innovation makes the end user's life better. Everything else is secondary. This is a message that resonates with and appeals to Google's team. Responding to it will help Google retain its dominant market position.

Emotional Targets

George Mallory, one of the most famous mountaineers of all time, said that he climbed Everest because it was there. Any garden-variety mountain climber can tell you that's not true. The reason people climb mountains is simple: reaching the top delivers a tremendous emotional payoff. The bigger the mountain, the bigger the thrill. Standing on top of Everest, you're literally on top of the world. Those who have been there describe the soaring spirit, the life-changing joy, and the personal triumph that accompany gaining the top as a peak experience. The feeling is so amazing, so exhilarating, and so over the top that it has been described as the ultimate addiction. Nothing makes you feel as good, and there's always another adventure to be had.

The final element of our Brand Vision map is to identify that emotional payout. What is the peak experience that your Brand Lovers are searching for? What is the compelling emotional experience that keeps them coming back to your brand, time and time again? What do they hope to experience?

Emotional expectations motivate us to begin a relationship with a brand. They're the reason we're willing to begin climbing the mountain. Those first steps in the foothills are critical. It is the nature and quality of the emotional payout that a customer experiences as a result of that early engagement that determine whether he stays with a brand, decides to take his business elsewhere, or, in the best-case scenario, falls in love with the brand. As consumers, we're perpetually in search of the ultimate, the pinnacle, the mountaintop experience. It's exhilaration that keeps us coming back.

Ideally, then, every engagement with the customer is a miniature expedition. We may not be traversing entirely new terrain, but we're definitely taking a journey together toward a desired emotional outcome. Whether it's an advertisement, packaging, the company website, a retail location, or a call to customer service, that peak experience (or the promise of it) must be present at the beginning of the exchange, remain constant throughout the interaction, and play a significant role in the customer's memory of the event afterward (even if the memory is unconscious). The stronger and more resonant the peak experience is for the Brand Lover, the more often she'll come back. It's as simple as that.

All brands have some sort of peak experience. It doesn't matter what type of industry you're in or what types of products or services you purvey. Your Brand Lovers choose to do business with you consistently in part because of the emotional payoff from the experience.

Hitting the Emotional Target

What is your brand's emotional payoff? What experience are your customers seeking from you? Dominant organizations succeed because they know and can clearly articulate what their best customers are seeking from them, experientially.

Google knows that its customers choose it because it provides superior search tools. More than that, it understands, and does everything possible to reinforce, the emotional experience of choosing Google. It appeals to the user who understands and wants a range of sophisticated web tools. It provides comfort and confidence by continuing to set the bar: there is an expectation that if Google creates a tool, it's a better tool.

HBO's emotional target is completely different. Google's customers are searching for safety, security, dependability, and sophistication. HBO's Brand Lovers will take the sophistication, but they're not at all interested in safety and security, at least where their television viewing is concerned. They want to be challenged, pushed, startled, and surprised. They value the edgy and dangerous. They're seeking an experience that can be scary and satisfying in equal measure.

The same person can be a Brand Lover of both Google and HBO. He's seeking different emotional payoffs for different roles in his life. To be able to find reliable information quickly online, the safety and sophistication of Google appeals. To be entertained and to have one's conventions challenged, HBO's daring approach is more appropriate. Identifying and delivering the emotional target your Brand Lovers are seeking is an essential element of Brand Vision.

Brand Vision: Providing Confidence and Eliminating Uncertainty

Combining the four components of Brand Vision provides us with a comprehensive understanding of what it takes to function as a dominant organization once we reach the top. We know who our best customers are and what their role is in our success. We understand clearly what the most critical aspects of our organization are and what it takes for the entire organization to work in a unified direction. A common purpose permeates every aspect of our operations, from the frontline employee to the CEO. Everyone is working within the same parameters. This is what it takes to make it to the top.

In today's competitive business environment, there is nothing more fatally expensive than distractions. Organizations that want to do more than survive cannot afford to take their eyes off the finish line. The parameters and borders imposed by a Brand Vision allow us to focus on what's most essential and important. If it doesn't get you closer to your planned success, it doesn't matter. This efficiency of thought is the hallmark of the dominant organization.

Brand Vision streamlines decision making tremendously. Before you go forward with an initiative, it must be checked through the lens of Brand Vision. Is this decision going to reinforce how your Brand Lovers see you? Are your actions in alignment with their expectations? What about your team's expectations? Google seldom receives harsher criticism than when it's perceived as doing something "evil." Your cultural values are always a critical consideration. You want the best people possible, and you want them to be eager and excited about being part of your team. Finally, most important, will this course of action deliver the peak experience your Brand Lovers demand?

Only when all these questions can be answered successfully can an organization move forward with an acceptable degree of confidence. Using Brand Vision eliminates uncertainty and reduces the risk of organizational decision making. You can zoom in on success, as long as all four components of Brand Vision are satisfied. (For an example of a completed Brand Vision statement, see Chapter 12.)

Where It Counts the Most

- Brand Vision makes your organization more efficient. Every decision can be weighed against a single criterion: does this choice move your company closer to your vision of success or further away from it?
- On the surface, customer behavior appears to be extremely dynamic and volatile. Brand Modeling provides the tools we need to delve more deeply and completely, going below the surface to identify the constant elements needed for success.
- Changes in our customers' personal, professional, or economic lives can affect the relationship they have with our brands. Dominant organizations understand the paramount pressures facing their best customers and how those pressures can change behavior.
- How do your best customers define themselves? Every organization should be able to answer this question with three accurate adjectives.
- Never forget that the way our best customers see themselves may be fundamentally different from our assumptions about our best customers. Remember, it's the Brand Lovers' perceptions that matter the most!
- Brand Lovers expect that the organizations they do business with will act in alignment with their own ideals and values.
- Dominant organizations win because they have a common purpose, a unity of vision that delivers meaningful rewards on every level: for the organization as a whole and for individual workers.
- All decision making must be in alignment with your organization's company culture. Going against your own values will alienate Brand Lovers and employees alike.

- Understanding and delivering the peak emotional experience is how dominant organizations win. This can mean changing the way your company has always done business or, in the case of truly dominant organizations, the way your industry operates.

PART IV

Deploying Your Model

CHAPTER 10

Activating the Insights of Your Brand Model

Recruiting Your Team: Who's Going to Help You Win?

Are you ready to get started? At this point, you're probably raring to go, eager to hit the ground running. After all, all you have to do is follow the lead of your Brand Lovers. Meeting the needs of these highly motivated, loyal, profitable customers is a sure route to the point where your company will enjoy unprecedented levels of profitability, free from meaningful direct competition. But first, there's one last task to be completed.

It's time to talk about your team—the people who will be making the journey toward ultimate profitability with you. You need the wholehearted support and enthusiastic participation of every member of your organization, from your colleagues at the conference table to the frontline employees who connect directly with your customers. In order to reach the mountaintop, every member of the team must be committed and equipped with the resources needed to make success possible.

This isn't optional. No man is an island, and business success is seldom a solo adventure. It doesn't matter what industry you're planning to dominate. You'll need a support team. They may be "off camera," receiving little, if any, of the attention, but they provide all of the vital elements that make success possible.

Aligning Your Leadership Team

Add evangelist to the list of jobs you have to perform. It's your role to convince your company's leaders that there is a better way for them to do what they've already been doing and, more than that, convince them to embrace the change with such contagious enthusiasm that rank-and-file employees follow suit.

Every company is different. Introducing the concepts of Brand Modeling may involve a simple refinement of what your organization has already been doing, or it may require a series of major corporate transitions over a period of time. Highlighting the benefits is essential, especially when you're talking to colleagues who understand the scale of the changes proposed and the impact they will have on your company. Yet these are the very people you need to have "buy into" your idea.

Joseph Campbell tells us that there are two reasons myths are created. The first is to keep people in the village, where they can be safe and productive. The second reason is to drive people out of the village, undertaking quests and challenges to garner great rewards. A wholehearted embrace of the second approach is necessary when you're talking with your leadership team. You want its members to embark on the hero's journey with you.

You're presenting the members of your leadership team with a real challenge. Are they ready to take their brand message seriously? Understanding that a sense of fun is important to your best customers is one thing. Appointing a chief-level director of fun to make sure that a sense of fun permeates every aspect of the customer's experience is another. Providing that director with a budget and a staff to transform theory into reality is still another. Where does your team stand on the continuum of commitment?

The Life is good Company committed its organization to optimism. Zappos chose happiness. Whether that manifests as coffee mugs with quirky logos or drop-dead sexy heels doesn't matter nearly as much as delivering the emotional impact—the peak experience—that the customer expects from the brand.

Your organization can do the same, especially if you have a supportive, enthusiastic, skilled team working with you.

Step Up like Shackleton

Leaders guide by example, continually demonstrating not only where the organization is going, but how the journey will be made. With their actions, strong leaders model the behavior that they want to see—that they need to see—from everyone who is embarking on this adventure with them. They exemplify the qualities they value most from their team.

In other words, you need to "be the change you want to see" in the organization. It is your role and your duty to provide an example. You're showing your team how it needs to perform in both good circumstances and bad.

Modeling the behavior you want to see when events are working favorably and your team is making good progress is important. You're developing a culture of trust within your organization. The success of any company is based on the faith that the team has in its leadership. As long as the team members have confidence that there's someone in charge who knows where he's going and the best way to get there, they'll keep doing their part.

If that confidence wavers, however, team members begin to worry about their own safety and security. They begin to look for their own way up to the top, or even back down. They hoard resources and energy, uncertain that the leaders will allocate them appropriately. These behaviors can signal the death knell for any organization. Without unity of purpose, it is impossible for a company to be successful.

The leader's steps to build confidence bear fruit in many ways. First and foremost, strong leadership helps to unify the expedition behind a single, compelling vision. The distractions and associated destructive behaviors are eliminated. Most important, building confidence within the ranks when things are going well helps an organization's employees trust in and follow that leadership when things go badly.

It was Ernest Shackleton's performance as leader of the Nimrod Expedition, and his subsequent success discovering the Furthest South point, that persuaded men to join his team in the historic race to the South Pole. Shackleton lost that race, but the faith in his leadership and his ability to bring an Antarctic expedition team safely home stood him well on his next adventure, the 1914 Imperial Trans-Antarctic Expedition. When Shackleton's ship, the *Endurance*, was trapped in pack ice, it was essential that his men trust him absolutely and implicitly. That was the only way safety could be reached—it was long, long before the days of rescue helicopters and GPS tracking! Based on Shackleton's word that he'd get his people home, the crew followed him over treacherous ice, frozen seas, and some of the world's harshest terrain. The trust paid off, and they all made it home alive.

Will your team follow you if pack ice engulfs your ship? Being a leader means acknowledging pragmatic concerns. You must be aware that catastrophe is always waiting in the wings. Unforeseen circumstances can throw the most carefully crafted itinerary into complete disarray. Witness BP's oil spill or Toyota's sticky accelerator issue. Dominant organizations benefit from having leaders that the employees have justified confidence in. They are resilient, adaptable, and responsive—all essential elements for responding to and overcoming business crises.

Strategies for Selling In

The tenets of Brand Modeling that can be used to find the best way to a dominant position in the marketplace, providing valuable guidance when selling your new direction to your employees.

Good leaders understand what makes people want to follow them. This requires a high degree of social intelligence, along with a strong understanding of what motivates people, both within their organizations and in general. Knowing who your audience is and what resonates with it the most provides the route to successfully introducing change into an organization.

Any change can be implemented successfully as long as your team members continue to receive the tangible and emotional rewards they expect from their relationship with your organization. What we're talking about is your employees' version of the peak experience.

Once you've identified what that peak experience is, it's time for strategic thinking. Your goal is to determine how to provide that peak experience for both your Brand Lovers and your employees. Revealing to your employees how their expectations of a peak experience are related to your Brand Lovers' peak experiences is critical. Articulating that relationship continually, in a way that's crystal clear, lets your team members know what's expected of them and why their contribution is important. At the end of the day, everyone needs to be in alignment, working toward a common goal. Your job as leader is to keep everyone all lined up and moving in the right direction.

Here are some strategies you can use to make that happen.

Begin with Your Brand Lovers: Creating a Customer Definition

Brand Modeling teaches us that the route to success is understanding and meeting the needs of your Brand Lovers. They serve as guides, leading your organization to increased profitability as they search for increasingly higher levels of fulfillment. Brand Lovers are critically important to your organization's success. Shouldn't your team members know who they are?

Define your best customers for your employees. Let them know who your most profitable, most loyal customers are. Describe your Brand Lovers as completely as possible. When you give your customers more dimension and depth, your team members will have more empathy for those customers. They'll be able to identify ways in which they are like your customers, places where their interests can align naturally.

Take steps to ensure that your employees understand that organizational success rests directly on serving your Brand Lovers well. Make it clear that every point of contact is an opportunity to reinforce the bond between your company and your Brand Lovers. No one's job is too small or insignificant to matter. Everyone has the potential to make the Brand Lovers love you more.

Inspire Through Conversation

Winston Churchill had to rally a small, battered nation that had endured devastating losses to keep fighting, even when the chances for victory seemed slim. Centuries earlier, King Henry V had needed men to fight for him at Agincourt, a battle that appeared guaranteed to be a bloodbath. Both men embraced the power of oratory, using compelling narratives to inspire phenomenal results in the face of overpowering odds.

We can learn from these examples. Inspiring your employees with the power of your words is a powerful tool. Speaking with passion and conviction about your vision for the organization and the growth you'll be experiencing, to the people who are going to make it happen, is essential for buy-in. You'll be converting your team to a fairly radical business approach. Now you'll be basing your organizational choices upon the wants and needs of your business's best customers. This isn't an endeavor that you can go about with a lackluster attitude or a sense of business as usual. You need passionate believers, zealous to create a new success in the world.

You can create these passionate believers by having inspirational conversations in group settings: conventions, conferences, and meetings. Reaching many people at once is efficient, encourages a sense of group identity, and can boost organizational energy levels and morale.

Equally as important are the conversations you have one on one. Speaking with your management team and other key employees regularly about the journey the company is making, including assessments of progress, and restating the goals and visions will help the message reverberate down through the ranks.

Show that you're paying attention. Get away from the corporate office and talk to frontline staff. The last thing you can afford at this point is artificial hierarchies in your company structure. Your success is dependent upon how well your frontline employees implement the new Brand Vision. Isn't it worth spending the time to make sure your team knows exactly what that vision is and what it means? Conversations with your people provide inspiration, guidance, and motivation, all of which are essential elements of buy-in.

Teach Your Teams: Become a Walking Presentation

A critical component of any endeavor is educating the team about what to expect from the coming adventure. Edmund Hillary talked to his team about the conditions on Everest. They knew what kind of terrain and what challenges they could expect along the way. Ernest Shackleton ensured that everyone who went to the Antarctic with him knew what he was getting into and that everyone was equipped to survive the journey. In the same way, as a leader, you want to prepare your employees with appropriate information, so they're ready and able to perform at top levels.

What is the best way to educate your employees? Don't just write stuff down in a memo and expect your team members to do something with it. When you write something down, it dies. Lifeless words on a page aren't going to get your employees fired up and engaged with your new approach. You have to do more than that. Generating enthusiasm requires a more theatrical approach. People need to see your enthusiasm and excitement. They need to see that same enthusiasm and excitement mirrored by colleagues and coworkers that they trust. Recruit evangelists— people who believe in your vision and can articulate it well—to spread the message.

A critical component of this education is letting your employees know what's in it for them. Remember that we're all always searching for that peak experience. What does that mean in the context of your employees' life? Let them know what cool things are on the way. They need to hear what type of awesomeness they can expect. Embrace media heavily here. Images that can be seen and stories that can be heard are infinitely more powerful than any photocopied memo or e-mail that can be filed away and disregarded. Never underestimate the power of images to communicate emotional messages. Showing your employees what life will be like when the company is on top is even more powerful than telling them.

Bring the Brand to Life

Nothing sells like success. The need to belong is a compelling psychological motivator, and belonging to a winning organization is even more attractive. Let your team members know how well they're doing. Let them know regularly and often that your best customers choose your organization first for a reason—them!

Having clearly articulated points of pride can play a critical role in your employees' peak experience. Sales data and performance reports are all well and good, but objective benchmarks just aren't enough. Employees are motivated by more than logic. They need compelling emotional reasons to turn in top performances. A psychological paycheck is just as important as monetary compensation.

Give your brand's success a voice. Use that voice to talk to your employees, and make that conversation all about the psychological payoff your employees are searching for. Find ways to showcase your success for your employees. Create a video that features happy customers. Is there a bigger ego boost than people lining up to come into the store you work for? There is valuable social currency associated with working for a dominant organization. And if your organization is a serious up-and-comer, poised to become the next company on top? That carries some serious cultural cachet as well. Give your employees opportunities to revel in their association with you.

Let your employees hear directly from the customers who are driving your success. People connect to people. Your Brand Lovers can be a great source of inspiration and motivation. Who better to talk about your organization than the people who love it most? Let your employees see whom they are working to satisfy. Post pictures of your best customers around the office, reinforcing the fact that there are real, live people who enjoy and appreciate the work you do. Pass on compliments from clients to the entire staff. Social media are powerful tools. Something as simple as awarding the "Best Tweet of the Week" can provide the subtle, constant positive reinforcement that dominant organizations need if they are to thrive.

Bring Your Customer to Life

Bringing your employees' goals into alignment with your Brand Lovers' goals is easier when your employees know who your Brand Lovers are. We're searching for a deeper understanding here, a familiarity with who your best customers are as people. We need insights deeper than those that can be reduced to a handful of psychological and demographic characteristics.

There's no more effective way to accomplish this than to have your employees spend time—actual, physical time—with your Brand Lovers. Experience is the best teacher. Theory is all very well and good, and you can give motivational speeches all day long, but nothing will get your employees on board with your expedition more effectively and efficiently than direct interaction with your best customers.

Spending a day on the open road with the members of the local HOG chapter will give any Harley-Davidson employee a new, deeper understanding of what it means to own a Harley. She'll see firsthand what motivates people to buy Harley's bikes, and what role having a Harley plays in their life. When it's time to get back to work—whether that's on the manufacturing line, on the sales floor, or in administration and support—that employee will benefit from a deeper understanding of what it is she's doing.

Seeing how your brand exists in the "real world" can be a transformative experience for your team members. Whether that means arranging tours of manufacturing plants so your team can see the gear they build in action or hosting events like Ben & Jerry's popular Free Scoop Day, do what it takes to get your employees and your best customers in the same place at the same time.

Emphasize the Connection

Your team members need to know who your customers are. More than that, they need to know how they connect with your

Brand Lovers on an individual basis. We're looking for specific, precise details here. Every single employee needs to know, in a very real and concrete way, how his daily efforts affect the lives of your Brand Lovers. How does what each employee does make a difference?

Obviously, this answer will vary with the employee's position. Sometimes the connection is obvious. The tech working at Apple's Genius Bar is there to witness that pivotal moment when the customer gets it and learns how to make her latest purchase perform its iMagic. The value in the relationship is immediately obvious to both the Brand Lover and the employee.

Other times, finding the connection isn't as easy. Even the most devoted Brand Lover might not be aware of the employee's existence. Tracing a direct line from the HR administrator's assistant to the devoted Coach bag buyer will be tricky, for example. The leader's role is to provide illumination and reinforce the role that every employee plays in fulfilling the brand's promise to its customers. It must be explicitly clear that your organization exists to serve the Brand Lovers, helping them realize their peak experience, time and time again.

What IKEA Does Right

IKEA dominates the modern home design market. Some people would even say that IKEA *is* the modern home design market. IKEA's giant stores, filled with fun, quirky, build-it-yourself furniture and trendy yet tasteful accessories, set the standard. IKEA's Brand Lovers regularly report driving hours to shop at their favorite store, willingly camping out in parking lots, and sleeping on sidewalks for days when the chain hosts special events. (Watch our five-minute documentary of an IKEA grand opening, titled "IKEA: Cult Branding Done Right," at http://www.cultbranding.com/ikea-video.)

Examining IKEA's success reveals that the organization has made a significant commitment to its employee base. For every fan the store has shopping the aisles, one *BusinessWeek* reporter said, it has another fan working for it. IKEA's employees are passionate about their company, and it shows.

A strong sense of Swedish-tinged egalitarianism has permeated IKEA's culture from the earliest days. All employees are considered equally important to the company's success. Managers and regional directors regularly spend time "swapping jobs" with frontline employees so that they can experience loading trucks and selling mattresses.

IKEA provides significantly more training than any of its retail competitors. Although the company has recently come under criticism for offering U.S. manufacturing workers conditions that are less cushy than those enjoyed in hyperliberal Sweden, overall employee reviews include glowing references to a transparent management style, freedom to work without a script, and a genuine concern for employees' health and safety.

IKEA's leadership has adapted the quirky promotions that it uses to great effect to connect with customers to strengthen the bond the company has with its employees. Holiday gifts and bonuses are nothing new—but giving all of your employees a custom-designed, build-it-yourself, super-cool bike for the holidays? That's pure IKEA.

Although economic pressures have certainly flooded the marketplace with willing applicants, IKEA still goes to significant trouble to make sure its new hires are a good fit. People want to work for winning organizations. It's easy for potential employees to see themselves cheering for customers as they enter the store. Identifying and continually enriching the peak experience that IKEA employees value most about their career is an essential element in IKEA's success. It has a great team, and it makes sure that team knows that it is valued and appreciated.

Focus on the Front Line

You need your leaders to believe in the concepts of Brand Modeling. You need your frontline employees to implement them. Creating this sort of wide-scale buy-in, with enthusiastic support from rank-and-file employees, can be accomplished in a number of ways.

Companies that have the will can take any of the strategies outlined previously and develop them into effective tools. Don't be afraid to embrace the theatrical. You need to reach people's hearts and minds. Transform your employees' expectations. Stage training exercises, play war games, or treat the operation as if you were opening a play on Broadway. Giving your team members things to be excited about, coupled with the real, pervasive sense that what they're doing makes a real, concrete difference in the company's success is a powerhouse combination. We all want to have a good time—but more than that, we want to matter. The same biological drivers that motivate our customers persuade our employees to get out of bed and come to work in the morning.

Where It Counts the Most

- Buy-in from your leadership is essential. Embracing Brand Modeling, especially its underlying premise that ultimate success lies in meeting the wants and needs of your Brand Lovers above all else, may require major organizational changes.
- Commitment exists along a continuum; you may have leadership support that is hesitant at first. As success builds on success, you'll see the enthusiasm grow.
- Be the change you want to see within your organization. Model the behavior you want your team to have. If you want to be known as the friendly company, you'd better be friendly!
- Dominant organizations win by connecting their employees with their Brand Lovers in direct and meaningful ways. Every point of contact is an opportunity to reinforce the bond between your organization and your best customers.
- Generating excitement requires a theatrical approach. Use all the tools you have at your disposal to capture your employees' attention, win their hearts, and harness their enthusiasm.
- Go beyond words: images, iconography, and symbols can help make the message more meaningful for your team members.
- Being part of a successful organization is a peak emotional experience in and of itself. People want to be proud of the work they do. This humanistic driver should never be underestimated.
- The most important question an employee needs to ask at the beginning of every day is, "How will I make a difference in our Brand Lovers' lives today?"

- Dominant organizations have fans among their employees as well as in the general public. Enthusiastic employees believe in your Brand Vision and do their part to make it happen.
- Dominant organizations are extremely selective about whom they hire. Great employees are key to delivering superior service to Brand Lovers.

CHAPTER 11

Living the Model

What We Expect from Ourselves: Adhering to the Brand Model

Developing a great Brand Model for your business takes time. Investing significant amounts of resources into understanding the wants, needs, and desires of your Brand Lovers provides you with a valuable tool that can guide your business to a point of greater profitability and heightened efficiency. But crafting and implementing the Brand Model are only the beginning. To be successful, you must *adhere* to your Brand Model.

What does it mean to adhere to your Brand Model? For one thing, you must remain committed to understanding who your Brand Lovers are. The success of your organization depends on your ability to connect effectively with your Brand Lovers. If you continually shift your attention from one group of customers to another, declaring each of them to be your Brand Lovers du jour, you will never be able to form effective connections. This will result in a dilution of your brand.

Constancy Is the Key to a Sure Footing

Adidas gives us a great example of the role of constancy in brand success. The German sneaker manufacturer made a brilliant strategic decision when it approached Jesse Owens with a sponsorship deal. The world had yet to develop the sports-centric culture that exists now, but it had its eyes firmly fixed on those Olympic Games and Owens's spectacular performance. The next triumph came when Adidas provided the shoes for the underdog West German soccer team. When the team won, Adidas sailed to the top of the soccer shoes market.

Had Adidas remained focused on best serving the needs of serious athletes, particularly soccer players, it would have remained a leading footwear company. Sports culture has exploded in the half century since Adidas's founding. In that time, however, Adidas went astray. Its shoes became popular for a while among the rap community, particularly after the brand was embraced by Run-DMC. Diverting its attention from its primary market took Adidas away from its core business, and the athletes who needed and valued high-performance shoes took their business elsewhere. Today, Adidas lags behind Nike, which has kept its focus on producing shoes that help athletes win.

If you want to reach the mountaintop, you have to stick to the trail. You can't just go wandering off in random directions and hope that you'll eventually reach the top. Adidas had made a phenomenal start up the mountain, but it became distracted. Losing its direction—failing to be aware of and best serve the needs of its Brand Lovers—resulted in a lot of wasted time, energy, market share, and profitability.

The Merits of Measurement

Adhering to your Brand Model means making a commitment to continually being aware of and responsive to your Brand Lovers.

This constancy matters. Measuring and understanding the influences shaping Brand Lovers' behavior also provides organizations with information on what they need to do to become and remain dominant in the marketplace: a tantalizing glimpse of the next mountaintop. The best business leaders have a need to know that there's always another challenge. They are happier, and they function best, when there's always another market to conquer, another goal to reach. The more specific and enticing that challenge appears, the more your leadership will find it irresistible.

Great companies are not built by the spectators of business. You can't achieve greatness sitting on the sidelines. You have to be there, on the playing field, lining up against the biggest linebackers you've ever seen, ready to power through and gain, inch by inch if necessary, the yards needed to make that first down. Endurance and commitment matter. People need a reason to hang in there. The first down may be exhilarating, but you haven't yet made a touchdown. You haven't yet won the game. Great players have a vision in their minds of what victory will look like. That keeps them going.

Continually monitoring and measuring your Brand Lovers provides the material that your organization needs in order to craft its own image of victory. There is great value to be found in spending time with your customers. Every single point of engagement is a teaching moment, where your customers are educating you in the way they'd like to be served. Each organization will develop its own unique approach, but here are some tools that dominant organizations have been successfully using to stay connected to their Brand Lovers:

- *Events.* Special events, such as Harley's HOG gatherings, give dominant organizations an ideal way to spend time with their best customers, learning what excites and inspires them. Successful events foster the sense of community and connection that Brand Lovers have built around your organization.

- *Social media.* Social media have made it much easier to talk with your customers. Pay attention to what's happening on your organization's social media platforms. Go beyond the mindless drive to have the most fans of your Facebook page. Instead, actively invite interaction, and your customers will provide valuable guidance about what they'd like to see from your organization. Weta Workshop, one of the world's premier producers of licensed figurines and action figures for science fiction and fantasy movies (and the artistic geniuses behind all of the props in *Lord of the Rings*), regularly asks its fan base which figurines it would like to see created next. American Girl Dolls, a dominant player in the competitive doll market, uses its "Doll of the Year" contest to determine which new dolls to introduce to its fanatically loyal customer base.

- *Customer content.* Embrace any opportunity to tap into your Brand Lovers' creativity. Consumer-generated content can be a little rough around the edges: witness the quirky YouTube videos that dominated the web when Cheetos was searching for its next big campaign. Popular videos were forwarded almost endlessly, and fans voted for the ad they most wanted to see during the Super Bowl. Was the ad itself successful? The tremendous participation rates and enthusiasm for the project strengthened Brand Lovers' attachment to their favorite crunchy orange snacks, and the sense of community and fun attracted new customers to the brand. It's not all necessarily kitsch out there, either. In fact, your Brand Lovers just might be geniuses. Canon really "got the picture" when it joined forces with director Ron Howard for its Project Imagin8ion campaign. Participants were invited to send in their best pictures. Eight of these images were

selected to influence Ron Howard's next film. It's an irresistible offer for would-be auteurs.
- *Measurement.* Measure everything you can measure. The
hard numbers gathered from strategic analysis of your
POS and sales data provide the objective perspective necessary to validate and support what your Brand Lovers
are telling you.

You can know what's possible only when you know what
you've already got and how much potential is inherent in the
passions of your Brand Lovers. Great leaders will be tremendously excited by this, and that excitement is the lifeblood of
dominant organizations. Enthusiasm is contagious, particularly
when it's partnered with effective science and proven results.

Don't Send Your Brand Up in Smoke: The Sweet Smell of Zippo?

If we were to extrapolate about Zippo's Brand Lovers, we'd say the
biggest fans of the lighters valued Zippo's quality, reliability, and
all-American appeal. However, this same extrapolation probably
won't indicate any particular fondness for Zippo's scent. No one
buys lighter fluid because he likes the smell. We're not even
sure that olfactory considerations make it onto the radar where
Zippo's Brand Lovers are concerned.

And even if the smell of a Zippo lighter is a powerful touch
point for the brand's best customers, there's no evidence that this
will translate to perfume. Experiencing a scent as an inherent
part of the product experience doesn't mean that people will
want to wear that smell themselves.

That didn't stop Zippo from introducing its own line of fragrance. The scent is called "Zippo Original" (and not, as more
than a few comic wits suggested, "Arson"). Whether the perfume
is appealing on its own merits doesn't matter. What we're

concerned about is whether this new direction is likely to do anything positive for Zippo's relationship with its Brand Lovers.

We're guessing that it won't. It's pretty likely that the whole Zippo fragrance idea will go up in smoke. The key issue comes down to consistency—is a Zippo perfume *consistent* with the company's Brand Lovers' ideal experience with Zippo?

There are circumstances in which offering a fragrance is a natural brand extension. For example, take Victoria's Secret. When the lingerie retailer offered its first fragrance, customers embraced it with open arms. The Victoria's Secret scent line has been a strong performer for the company from day one. That's not surprising. Customers who come to Victoria's Secret are heavily invested in making themselves look and feel sexy. Perfume is also often about looking and feeling sexy. Customers discovering fragrance options from Victoria's Secret were finding that the company had made a way to make their experience— both in the store and after they got home—even better. The alignment is obviously there.

When we consider the same situation with Zippo, however, there's no natural fit. The best customers of Zippo and Victoria's Secret might both indeed be trying to start fires—Zippo Original even promises to help you "light your passions"—but the latter is doing so only in a metaphorical sense. Consistency makes all the difference.

Adhering to the Brand Model when Things Go Wrong

It's easy to stick to a Brand Model when everything's going right. The real test of the system happens when things go wrong. Challenges crop up for every organization. The heightened awareness you have of your Brand Lovers can make it easier for you to spot a problem before it reaches its full magnitude, enabling you to take corrective action quickly.

And if something slips under the radar or arrives so suddenly that there's no time to head the problem off at the pass? Brand Modeling serves as a guide for crisis management. Consider how your Brand Lovers would expect you to resolve the situation. There aren't any simple answers. The more insights and information you have about your Brand Lovers, the more likely you are to craft solutions that meet and exceed your best customers' expectations.

The 1970s were a tumultuous time in our country. They were a disaster for Harley-Davidson. People who loved the brand, including pivotal members of Harley's leadership team, knew what the company's best customers wanted. They also knew that the company wasn't delivering it. Bikes from what are now darkly referred to as the AMF years had very unflattering nicknames. The Hardly Ableson and Hardly Drivable are two that we can actually print.

Delivering what Harley's Brand Lovers wanted required a major organizational change. It took an $80 million buyout by the firm's executives. Major, companywide changes were made. Quality was put back into the manufacturing process. The brand moved back toward the old-school look that its best customers loved.

Putting the focus back on what Harley's Brand Lovers wanted and expected from the brand wasn't easy. It took years for the company to regain market share and shine up a very tarnished reputation. You wouldn't know that today, however. Harley-Davidson has legions of loyal fans, and no one says the bikes are Hardly Drivable anymore.

Asking the Hard Questions:
What to Ask and When

Adopting Brand Modeling means focusing your entire organization on meeting the needs of your Brand Lovers. This will often require sweeping institutional change. Some things will need to be done better—and some things won't need to be done at all anymore. To put it bluntly, "What has to die?" (See the video here: http://www.cultbranding.com/what-has-to-die.)

To explain this to your team members, ask them to imagine your business as a garden. And in this garden, you grow only one thing: Brand Lover happiness. A successful garden yields bountiful crops. The more abundant your harvest of Brand Lover happiness, the more successful your organization is going to be. That's why the company has decided to pour every resource available into nurturing and cultivating this garden.

The more time, energy, and resources you put into your garden, the greater the crop yield is going to be. If you want a great harvest, there are tasks that must be performed. You have to water the garden. You have to feed the plants fertilizer so that they can thrive. In much the same way, you nurture your crop of Brand Lover happiness by watering it with continual customer contact, steadily monitoring your Brand Lovers, and taking great interest in what is meaningful to them. When you're right there, meeting and surpassing your Brand Lovers' expectations, you're providing the richest sort of fertilizer. Brand Lover happiness thrives under these conditions.

Feeding your crops may mean making significant changes in the way you do business. Let's say your Brand Lovers value honesty and transparency—things that we know are important to Southwest Airline's Brand Lovers. If you want to make your company more appealing to your Brand Lovers, you have to take steps that demonstrate your honesty and transparency.

How does Southwest do it? One thing it does is write all of its financial statements and reports at an eighth-grade reading level. Everyone within the organization can read and understand those reports. Nothing is hidden behind complex financial jargon that might be beyond a baggage clerk or flight line mechanic.

Southwest said it wanted everyone who works for it to know how well the company is doing—and it took real, meaningful steps to make this happen. That type of change helps achieve organizational buy-in. It also provides a compelling demonstration of core values to anyone who cares to delve deeply into the organization's operations. The change brought Southwest more into alignment with its Brand Lovers' expectations, and that is always a good thing.

Another critical garden task is weeding. Good gardeners know that weeds are a real challenge to crops. They sap away resources, stealing more than their fair share of sunlight and leaching your crop's much-needed minerals and nutrients out of the soil beneath their roots. Competing with the weeds is an impediment to your crop's optimum growth.

Recognizing weeds in a garden isn't difficult. Recognizing the weeds within our organization can be a lot more challenging. What needs to be "pulled out" and eliminated to encourage the growth of Brand Lover happiness?

The tough but true answer is, everything that has to. Any aspect of your business that isn't directly and concretely contributing to your Brand Lovers' happiness needs to go. These items often arise out of what we call *operant marketing*, or doing business the way you've always done business. Policies and procedures that may have made perfect business sense at one time are often continued long beyond the point where they're relevant or meaningful to your customers. We continue to do things because they've become habitual, unchanging, and unquestioned elements of how we operate.

Operant marketing is like chain smoking. You've developed a habit that will, inevitably and painfully, kill you. If you quit smoking, you can regain at least a fraction of the years you were burning away. And if you quit operant marketing, you just might wind up like Apple.

In 1996, Steve Jobs returned to Apple. The company he had founded was in bad shape. Under the leadership of Gil Amelio, Apple had explored many, many directions. The approach was always the same: any avenue that appeared to be profitable was explored with great enthusiasm, leaving Apple diluted and poorly defined to the public.

Jobs brought the focus back to what Apple's best customers wanted most. The company's bloated structure was slashed dramatically. At one point, Apple's product line boasted 350 items. Jobs cut this down to 10 items, but each of those items needed to be as close to perfect as possible.

The formula worked. Apple Brand Lovers aren't mourning the 340 products that Apple doesn't sell anymore. They're having the time of their lives with those that remain. Jobs kept only the best. And then the company focused on making the best better.

Brand Modeling has given us the ability to recognize who our Brand Lovers are and what they value the most. We know what our crop of Brand Lover happiness should look like. Armed with that knowledge, it becomes easier to see what needs to be pulled out. Reorganizing your business around the insights you've learned from your customers puts you in a position where you have to take a hard look at everything you do, but now you know what you're looking for.

It comes down to keeping the crops and pulling the weeds. Those aspects of your business that contribute to Brand Lover happiness can stay, although you know that they will have to change and evolve to better meet Brand Lovers' expectations over the course of time. Those aspects of your business that don't contribute to Brand Lover happiness need to be yanked out by the roots.

Steve Jobs did his share of yanking. Reducing Apple's product line meant closing several divisions that were underperforming or just too off message. The casualties included OpenDoc, Cyberdog, and Newton. Some of the choices you'll be forced to make will be controversial. The press at the time eviscerated Jobs over the changes he made to licensing agreements, effectively putting any company that wanted to make Mac clones out of business. It was a move that cost the company revenue at a time when it really needed to up its revenue streams. Today, however, Apple has no viable competition for the Mac, and the company's financial position is stronger than ever.

It takes a special sort of courage to be a good gardener. Imposing your will on nature in order to produce a desired crop or a pleasing landscape requires determination and consistency. In much the same way, it is at this point that an organization needs to be willing to question everything. There can be no sacred cows. Radical change can be frightening, particularly in companies with deeply entrenched nonproductive systems. The best way to alleviate the pain of what doesn't work is to showcase the success that results when all of your organization's energies are focused on growing Brand Lover happiness.

Making Changes or Changing the Model?

Change can be uncomfortable, and it's never easy. The more profound and sweeping the change, the more resistance it will encounter. This is one of the fundamental truths of human nature that has been plaguing leaders for centuries. Machiavelli, in his masterwork, *The Prince*, said it very well: "There is nothing more difficult to take in hand, more perilous to conduct, or more uncertain in its success, than to take the lead in the introduction of a new order of things. For the reformer has enemies in all those who profit by the old order, and only lukewarm defenders in all those who would profit by the new order, this lukewarmness arising partly from fear of their adversaries . . . and partly from the incredulity of mankind, who do not truly believe in anything new until they have had actual experience of it."

In other words, you may face a challenge introducing your organization to the concepts of Brand Modeling. The tricky bit is to keep the relationship going, especially in the face of entrenched resistance. This requires both courage and caution from the leadership. You are well served if you know what type of obstacles may lie in your company's pathway to greatness.

One of the common responses to organizational change is to question the motivation behind the change. The model itself may be held up to special scrutiny.

This is a good thing. If we learned anything from Edwards Deming and his groundbreaking work studying the strengths of Japanese automobile manufacturers, it's that we never truly arrive at greatness. We become better businesses by making the journey. As we develop Brand Models, we facilitate meaningful change that delivers exceptional results by focusing exhaustively and exclusively on the needs of our best customers.

For most organizations, this is a major cultural shift. You can't make this type of change simply by putting up posters with catchy mottos or by paying lip service to the latest mission statement that sounds great but is ultimately devoid of meaning. You have to move beyond the trappings of change into actual metamorphosis.

That's what Deming did. He brought Ford back from the brink by instituting radical, organization-wide change. We're engaged in the same pursuit. The goal is not to create a new organizational doctrine that employees blindly follow. We need our teams to be invested and engaged in serving our Brand Lovers. Everything must be open to question, including the model itself. When the questions come, it's essential that we avoid becoming defensive and guarded. The Brand Model is a lens that allows us to examine and question customer behavior. It keeps us from falling into the business-killing trap of fundamentalist thinking.

We're talking about making a major shift in the overall culture of your organization. The questions are a great sign, because they show that your people are engaged and involved. They're confident enough to ask questions without fear. They're interested, even if they're resistant. This is the point where communication is vital. Striving for transparency and openness with your team will yield large rewards, especially when the people on the ground see the results.

Tracking and monitoring your Brand Lovers' responses to what you're doing creates a great accountability system. Let's say we have customer comments that a given retail location is not as clean as it might be—information that Kmart, for example, could have been listening to. When that information is reviewed, action steps are identified, and the manager of that location is given specific tasks to carry out to improve the situation. Improving the situation may seem like a minor step, but given time, the people in your organization will see the cumulative effects of these minor changes that bring you into alignment with your best customers' expectations.

So will your Brand Lovers, and their positive response will provide the much-needed energy and positive reinforcement required to keep your team engaged with and enthusiastic about the changes that are being made.

Where It Counts the Most

- Constancy is essential for brand success. When you identify the things that Brand Lovers love most about your organization, do not abandon those things.
- Without constant focus on your Brand Lovers, it becomes easy to lose direction, engage in unprofitable campaigns, and, worse, risk alienating your Brand Lovers.
- Knowing what resources and brand equity you already have gives you a much better sense of what's possible and what route you need to take to get there.
- Every point of customer engagement is a teaching moment: our customers teach us about the way they'd like to be served.
- Dominant organizations win because they know what their Brand Lovers expect from them. Some things will be a "natural fit," such as the Victoria's Secret fragrance line, while other initiatives might not work as well. Brand Modeling helps you discern which ideas are great and which ones are nonstarters.
- Campaigns that leave your Brand Lovers neutral at best are not helping your organization move toward the dominant position. Worse, you incur an opportunity cost: what could you have been doing with that time, energy, and resources to strengthen your bond with your Brand Lovers?
- Every organization has problems and will face challenges. Brand Modeling dictates that we find resolutions to these problems that keep our organization squarely in alignment with the expectations of our Brand Lovers.
- The more comprehensive and exhaustive your knowledge of your Brand Lovers is, the more satisfying the solutions you'll be able to craft to challenges and crises.

- Dominant organizations win because they're willing to question everything. There's no such thing as "we've always done it this way" anymore.
- Eliminate functions, initiatives, and protocols that don't move your organization closer to your Brand Vision. This introduces the efficiency that is essential for success.

CHAPTER 12

Bringing It All Together: A Sample Brand Model

FRESH ROASTED REVERENCE: A CASE STUDY

It's early on a Sunday morning. The sun is bright, and it promises to be a beautiful day. The coffee shop is nearly empty, with only a few tables occupied, so you don't feel bad about indulging in a leisurely conversation with the barista about your coffee preferences. You learn which beans are best right now. When your coffee is delivered, it's in a perfectly designed, graceful yet substantial mug.

You choose a table near the window. A small fountain bubbles nearby, sending cold, clear water over river pebbles. As you sit, you realize that planters full of bamboo and tropical greenery have been strategically positioned to ensure your privacy. You're free to enjoy your coffee in peace. That's easy to do because it's the best coffee you've ever had. It's the ideal time to read the morning papers, or simply sit back and enjoy some quiet reflection.

People enter and leave the coffee shop as the morning goes on, but their presence is not disruptive. You never feel hurried. There's no sense that there are people waiting for you to finish up and get out so that they can have your table. You feel the tension melting out of your body as you have time to examine your thoughts in peace and serenity.

That's the Shifu experience. Shifu's Coffee Palace is headquartered in San Francisco, California. For more than 15 years, it's been serving the world's best coffee drinks in a serene meditation center. It's Zen meets coffee shop.

THE BRAND MODELING PROCESS

We're presenting this case study, focused on the admittedly fictional but definitely appealing Shifu's Coffee Palace, to give you a complete overview of the Brand Modeling process. At this point, we've looked at all of the components of Brand Modeling individually. Seeing the model as a whole makes it easier to understand how everything works, and how a strong Brand Model can be used to guide any company to a more dominant position in the marketplace.

Shifu's Coffee Palace has enjoyed remarkable success. Its distinctive peaceful sanctuary approach, along with a focus on artisanally crafted coffee drinks, has won it a loyal, large following in the city by the bay. This pleases CEO Bob Shifu, who sees the Coffee Palace's success as validation of both the contemplative lifestyle and the artisan's quest for perfection.

With this success come choices, opportunities that are available only to brands that have both the vision and resources to move boldly. Bob Shifu is considering multiple directions in which to grow the brand.

The first is a West Coast expansion. Should there be more Shifu's Coffee Palaces? A dozen potential locations have been picked out, from Seattle to San Diego. Faster growth would be possible if Shifu adopted a franchise model. This approach has some traction among Shifu's leadership team.

Areum Koh, head of product development, sees Shifu's future as headed in a different direction. She is strongly advocating getting Shifu-branded coffee beans into a retail setting. Her goal is to make a deal with one of the nation's largest grocery chains, putting Shifu head to head with the established market-leading brands Folgers and Maxwell House.

The growth potential is clearly there. Yet CEO Bob Shifu has hesitations. Is the Shifu experience truly replicable? Does the brand's appeal result at least in part from the unique character of San Francisco? Will Shifu transplant well to Cleveland? Will expanding into grocery stores build brand visibility and market share, or will the move dilute the brand equity and alienate customers who viewed Shifu as something special and unique—not just another item to be picked up on the weekly grocery run?

Brand Modeling is the best tool to answer these questions. By identifying Shifu's Brand Lovers and delving deeply into what makes the brand so appealing to them, it will be possible to extrapolate, with a high degree of certainty, the outcome of any proposed changes. If a move will strengthen the Brand Lovers' relationship with Shifu, it will show in terms of increased profitability and market share.

Here's what that process looks like.

SHIFU'S COFFEE PALACE'S BRAND MODEL

The first thing we'll look at is the elements of Shifu's Brand DNA.

Brand DNA

A thorough examination of the various elements of Shifu's Coffee Palace's Brand DNA is the first step in the process. The Brand DNA highlights the unconscious and subconscious motivations that drive your best customers to build a relationship with your brand.

During this phase, we will be looking at humanistic drivers, archetypal images, cultural stories, and emotional targets. (To review each of these concepts, turn to Chapter 6.)

Humanistic Drivers

Humanistic drivers are the innate needs that exist within every human being. Making sure that these needs are met motivates, consciously or otherwise, every decision that we make. When we look at humanistic drivers, we consider seven types of need, based on Maslow's hierarchy.

Physiological. The need to breathe, eat, sleep, drink, and perform bodily functions

Safety. The need to keep one's body, one's family, and one's possessions safe

Love and belonging. The need for family, friendship, and intimacy

External esteem. The need for respect and validation from others

Internal esteem. The need for respect and validation from one's self
Cognitive. The need for logic, problem solving, and fact recognition
Aesthetic. The need for beauty
Self-actualization. The need to fully know and realize one's potential

What We Learned. Every person on the planet has some or all of these needs, but not everyone has the same needs at the same intensity. By examining Shifu's Brand Lovers, we learned that they scored high in the areas of love and belonging, aesthetics, and self-actualization.

Why This Is Important. We know now that Shifu's best customers value a sense of affectionate community in their coffee shop experience. The setting and the experience must be aesthetically pleasing. This means incorporating beauty into every aspect of the operation, from site design to the choice of mugs used to hold the beverages. Shifu's best customers place a premium on creativity and expression. They value having a place that fosters creative thinking, as well as the creative artistic output of others. This extends to the artistic preparation of coffee beverages.

Archetypal Images

As the fundamental expression of your brand, the archetypal images reflect the spirit of your business. These primordial images activate the emotions that your Brand Lovers associate with your brand. It is imperative to know what evocative images Shifu's Brand Lovers picture when they think of the Coffee Palace.

What We Learned. Researching Shifu's Brand Lovers revealed a quartet of powerful archetypal images associated with the brand. These images are:

The Artist. Both creative and solitary, the Artist is focused on her own personal vision of perfection.
The Master. The Master excels at craftsmanship. Even the humblest endeavor is elevated and transformed through the skill used and the attention paid to detail.
The Philosopher. Making thought an art form, the Philosopher values contemplation and reflection.

The Sanga. The Sanga is a setting for a supportive, spiritual community. There is a sense of retreat or separation from the mundane concerns of the world.

Why This Is Important. These archetypal images tell us a great deal about Shifu's Brand Lovers' expectations. The Brand Lovers may see themselves as the Artist, valuing the space Shifu provides to foster inspiration and spark creativity.

They may also see the baristas as artists in their own right. This ties into their understanding and appreciation of the Master archetype. At Shifu's, every cup is a masterwork. Beverages are topped by a foam art specialist.

Shifu's Brand Lovers identify strongly with the image of the Philosopher. They enjoy contemplating the mysteries of life, the universe, and everything else. While many of Shifu's best customers enjoy solitude, the ability to access a congenial community effortlessly also appeals. Hence the Sanga archetype.

Through this process, we have identified several essential elements in Shifu's success. The focus on the Artist and Master archetypes means that we must hire only the most skilled, talented baristas, individuals who can transform a simple cup of Joe into a delicious bit of performance art. To honor both the Philosopher and Sanga archetypes, there must be a special focus on seating in site designs: it is essential to provide space for both individual contemplation and friendly community.

Cultural Stories

Every brand has its own cultural stories. These stories serve as the legend or fairy tale of your brand, revealing the tension that is resolved by the brand, while simultaneously satisfying the deeper archetypal images and humanistic drivers.

Understanding Shifu's cultural stories reveals how the brand's best customers view the coffee shop and their place as patrons.

What We Learned. Shifu's cultural story is a message that there is an attractive alternative to the cookie-cutter, overcommoditized coffee shop. It reveals much about Shifu's Brand Lovers' dissatisfaction with a commercialized world and the lack of a place for the special, thoughtful Artist and Philosopher.

Once upon a time, in a land where all coffee shops had become commercial and uncreative, an Artist emerged among the people who brought back an appreciation of the bean and the craft of coffee making. More than just a beverage, this was the creation of a new form of art. Those souls search for meaning found themselves attracted to this coffee artisan and his beautiful palace, finding not only a new way of perceiving coffee, but also a place to gather, to think, and to engage in dialogue on the meaning of life.

Why This Is Important. Shifu's cultural story reveals the importance of a separate space that is markedly different from the culture as a whole. Its Brand Lovers value the opportunity to "opt out" of everyday life and enter a space where beauty and craftsmanship are paramount concerns. According to this story, the search for meaning trumps the desire for mocha.

This insight appears to be in immediate conflict with any thoughts of chain building or franchise-style expansion. If what Shifu's Brand Lovers value most is the sense that the business exists somehow outside the normal tawdry trails of ordinary commerce, a rapid move to develop a ubiquitous presence could shatter that perception of specialness. However, it's always important to construct an entire model before making organization-changing decisions. Acting in the absence of full information is premature; what we want is a more complete understanding prior to making any choices.

Emotional Targets

Emotional Targets reveal the primary emotions that your Brand Lovers associate with your organization. These are the emotions that we want to evoke at every touch point. Doing so strengthens our relationship with our Brand Lovers, which leads to greater stability and profitability.

What We Learned. Researching Shifu's Brand Lovers revealed that they are seeking a quartet of powerful emotions: awe, peacefulness, connectedness, and comfort.

Why This Is Important. Every aspect of Shifu's operation must be directed at evoking one or more of these critical emotions. Creating an environment that prompts feelings of awe, peacefulness, connectedness, and comfort requires delving deeply into customer preferences and understanding the visual, auditory, and tactile stimuli that create those feelings. These feelings can also be influenced by staff interaction, policies and procedures, and more: every aspect of Shifu's must be open for examination to make sure that the emotional connections are consistently being made.

Brand Insights

Brand Insights represent the tip of your marketing spear, revealing psychological factors that influence your customers' associations with your brand. At this point, we're going to be looking at three items through Shifu's Brand Lovers' eyes: primary tensions, primary belief systems, and the ideal experience. (See Chapter 7 for more in-depth coverage of these concepts.)

Primary Tensions

Primary tensions are the problems, aggravations, and irritations that shape your customer's day. We're looking for ways in which your brand solves the problem, alleviates the aggravations, or makes the irritations not quite so irritating.

What We Learned. For Shifu's Brand Lovers, it's all about taking their time. The synthesis of statements from its Brand Lovers revealed the following tensions:

> *I'm tired of careless coffee making, noisy environments, and feeling like I have to leave as soon as I take my last sip of coffee. Most coffee shops cater to people in a rush. At Shifu's, drinking a work of art, I feel welcomed, surrounded by others who appreciate the present moment.*

Why This Is Important. Understanding primary tensions reveals, with pinpoint accuracy, why our customers are turning to us to solve their problems. Shifu thrives because it positions itself directly counter to these tensions. By providing a slower-paced, peaceful environment and catering to each individual customer, Shifu resolves its Brand Lovers' tensions. Any change that would reintroduce those tensions into the Shifu experience must, by definition, be a nonstarter.

Primary Belief Systems

Primary belief systems reveal what your Brand Lovers hold to be true about your organization. These beliefs can be positive or negative. It's important to know what these beliefs are, because they form the substance of your brand in the customer's mind.

What We Learned. Shifu's Brand Lovers have many positive beliefs about the Coffee Palace. These include:

Shifu selects the best beans from around the world.

I always enjoy a sense of peacefulness when I have my coffee.

The coffee is always exquisite, beautiful to look at and delicious to drink.

The coffee is roasted to perfection, never burnt or bitter.

I'm always welcomed and treated respectfully by the staff.

I never have to rush through my coffee.

I find others like me who appreciate high-quality coffee in a relaxing environment.

Why This Is Important. Primary beliefs are an important diagnostic tool for any business. If your Brand Lovers articulate one or more negative beliefs, you need to take action and correct those perceptions. Failing to do this can have catastrophic consequences—just ask Kmart (Chapter 6).

In Shifu's case, the primary beliefs are overwhelmingly positive. Think of them as strengths in your SWOT (strengths, weaknesses, opportunities, and threats) analysis. These positive beliefs bond you to your best customers. The relationship gets stronger every time Shifu acts in a way that reinforces and validates the belief system.

The Ideal Experience

When we consider the ideal experience, we're searching for your Brand Lovers' vision of a perfect business encounter. This is how your business would operate in a perfect world.

What We Learned. In a perfect world, Shifu's would be a peaceful, quiet retreat where customers can enjoy fine coffee, contemplation, and, if desired, amiable conversation. Aggregating the Brand Lovers' responses to questioning revealed this composite answer:

> *I enter Shifu's Coffee Palace on a late Saturday morning. There are many patrons, but I'm served within minutes. Taking Shifu's latest creation to a comfortable, plush chair, I sit back and forget about the cares of the world, listening to a serene waterfall in the background. There's no technology and no immediate demands. I can sit with a book or a journal, or simply contemplate life's meaning. I hear an interesting exchange by several nearby patrons. I engage in their discussion for an hour before purchasing a snack and then slipping back into a quiet calm.*

Why This Is Important. If you don't know what your customer's ideal experience is, it is impossible to know what to strive for. It is possible that you'll deliver an ideal experience wholly by chance. Many businesses have become successful by delivering something remarkably close to the ideal experience, simply through trial and error. The value of Brand Modeling lies in the clear articulation of the ideal, which can move an organization closer to the dominant market position more quickly.

Since Shifu now has a clear understanding of the experience that its Brand Lovers are seeking, it can take steps to ensure that that experience is delivered consistently.

Brand Ecosystem

The next step in the Brand Modeling process is examining the Brand Ecosystem. The Brand Ecosystem refers to the environment your organization operates in. What does your customer mix look like? Who are your largest competitors? What makes your Brand Lovers choose your business over any other?

We will be looking at three areas: the customer loyalty continuum, the competitive landscape, and drivers of choice. For a more in-depth examination of each of these concepts, see Chapters 5 and 8.

Customer Loyalty Continuum

Customer loyalty exists along the continuum. There are a wide range of relationships that individuals can have with your organization. At the apex, there are Brand Lovers—the highly profitable portion of your customer base that enthusiastically recommends your company to family and friends. There are also Brand Enthusiasts, who are generally favorable toward your company, but who lack the passionate fervor of the Brand Lovers. Brand Nomads have a neutral attitude; they are neither predisposed to do business with you nor inclined to avoid your company entirely. These customers can easily be swayed by factors like convenience and price. Brand Haters may do business with you, but they resent every moment of the process. As soon as they identify a viable alternative, they're jumping ship.

What We Learned. In researching Shifu's customer base, we discovered the following mix:

Brand Lovers	10%
Brand Enthusiasts	38%
Brand Nomads	44%
Brand Haters	8%

We also examined the perceptions of each portion of the customer mix. The results are as follows:

Haters. This place is for hippies.
Nomads. Solid coffee. Bit pricey. Similar to many coffee shops.
Enthusiasts. Really good coffee. Nice place to relax. Friendly faces.
Lovers. I feel at home. I belong here. The best coffee in the world. Amazing baristas. I can just sit here and talk for hours.

Why This Is Important. Understanding the mindset and perceptions of your customer base reveals opportunities to transform Brand Nomads and Brand Enthusiasts into Brand Lovers. This makes them more valuable customers, increasing your overall profitability.

It's important to look at the proportion of each category of customer in relation to the whole. It is in the nature of business that the majority of your customers are likely to be Brand Nomads or Brand Enthusiasts. The goal is to consistently and continually grow your ranks of Brand Lovers. Keep an eye on the percentage of Brand Haters: if this number starts to trend upward, you'll need to identify the reason why.

Competitive Landscape

Analyzing the competitive landscape means taking a critical look at your organization's direct competitors. The purpose of this exercise is to identify strengths that can be profitably emulated, pinpoint weaknesses where your brand may have a competitive advantage, and keep a watchful eye on points where competitors are encroaching on your market share.

What We Learned. The coffee shop market is crowded and complex. Shifu's has many well-established competitors. To do this type of analysis properly requires a fairly exhaustive analysis of each competitor. Here is a snapshot synopsis of what we learned about the other companies vying for dominance in the coffee sector:

Starbucks: Ubiquitous locations; stay as long as you want; wide selection; loyalty program.

Caribou Coffee: Eco-awareness; commitment to quality coffee; loyalty program.

Così: Table service; quality food; a complete dining experience; artisanal environment.

Dunkin' Donuts: Fast service; many locations; good coffee; quick meals; positioned for breakfast.

McDonald's: Fast service; many locations; quick meals.

Local coffee shops: Convenient location; comfortable environment.

Why This Is Important. Understanding the Brand Ecosystem allows Shifu to understand the position it occupies relative to other coffee providers in the customer's mind, identifying points of commonality (for example, Caribou

Coffee is the closest competitor in terms of fine coffee) and points of differentiation (Shifu's appreciates the world we live in, but does not promote eco-awareness in the same way as Caribou).

Drivers of Choice

After identifying the other companies in the competitive environment, the next step is discerning why a customer would choose those organizations rather than yours. These reasons are known as drivers of choice.

Drivers of choice vary by industry. In the coffee shop industry, the following were identified as potential drivers of choice: price, quality, customer service, location, environment, fair trade, community, and variety of foods/beverages.

What We Learned. Our hypothetical analysis revealed the following three factors to be the most important drivers of choice:

Location. Location is the number one driver of choice within the overall coffee shop category. People don't want to travel too far to get their favorite coffee.

Quality. The coffee drinker's taste continues to get more refined. The quality of the coffee beverage—both the bean and the processing of the beverage—is the second most important driver of choice. Customers may not be well versed in the terminology that articulates why one cup of coffee tastes better than another, but when they find a brand of coffee that they enjoy, they tend to stick with it.

Price: Because coffee is consumed on a regular basis, the price of coffee is very important to the coffee consumer.

Why This Is Important. While Shifu's flagship store has remained in the same location, any planned expansion will have to include the selection of new sites. These data reveal the importance of having a convenient location. At the same time, it is clear that remaining competitive on quality and price is essential as well.

Brand Differentiators

Examining the Brand Ecosystem allows us to identify where we fit in the marketplace. The next step is to analyze the differentiators objectively. Brand differentiators are those factors that make us stand out in the market and are particularly appealing to Brand Lovers.

There are four areas to consider. A touch point assessment looks at every point of customer engagement. Brand positioning, the brand promise, and messaging strategy focus on identifying and articulating exactly what makes a brand different and how that difference is communicated to the Brand Lover.

Touch Point Assessment

A touch point assessment examines every point of engagement your customers experience, and compares it to those provided by your direct competitors. This provides a valuable diagnostic tool, identifying areas for improvement. The process also highlights strengths that you can use to reinforce the bond between your organization and your customers.

What We Learned. Shifu's touch point assessment revealed the following:

Store experience	Excellent
Staff	Great
Packaging (cups, etc.)	Great
Coffee quality	Great
Website	Very good
Social media	Very good
Logo	Good
Advertising	Good
Loyalty card	Fair

Why This Is Important. Shifu's offers a superior store experience. The loyalty card, on the other hand, isn't quite as impressive. Brand Modeling provides a tool to reveal your shortcomings. It's important to remember that correcting those shortcomings must be done in such a way as to improve your Brand Lovers' perception of your company.

Brand Positioning

Brand positioning tells us the position the brand currently holds with your best customers and gives a compelling picture of how the brand plans to win future market share. This is a statement of how your customers see you, and what your company will look like as it grows and evolves.

What We Learned.   Shifu's brand positioning addresses who the brand's best customers are, what products and services are offered, and in what fashion they're delivered.

> For contemplative, refined coffee drinkers, Shifu's Coffee Palace is the premier coffee house that delivers a serene and aesthetically enchanting experience because only Shifu's is committed to creating the most inspiring beverages in a Zen-like environment.

Why This Is Important.   Shifu's brand positioning rearticulates many of the themes we heard when we examined the Brand DNA. This is a critical guidepost that Shifu's leadership can use when weighing expansion plans. To be successful, any brand extension must deliver that same sense of peace and artistic delight, coupled with some of the world's best coffee. If these criteria aren't delivered—or if the brand extension gives the impression that Shifu's is for someone other than the contemplative, refined coffee drinker—then there is the risk of going off-brand, alienating your best customers, and imperiling the market position it currently holds.

Brand Promise

The brand promise outlines the spoken and unspoken promises that your company has made to its best customers. Putting these promises in the center of your operating procedures is more than good business sense: it keeps the entire organization focused on serving your Brand Lovers better than anyone else can.

What We Learned. Shifu's set of brand promises focuses on two distinct areas: the coffee it serves, and the experience it provides so that its best customers can enjoy the coffee.

> *Promise 1.* We promise to always source the best-quality beans and use precise roasting methods.
> *Promise 2.* We promise to always let you take your time.
> *Promise 3.* We promise to always provide a serene environment.

Why This Is Important. Shifu's brand promises are in alignment with what its Brand Lovers value most about the Coffee Palace. It's always good to check this. Your organization can promise fabulous things, but if they're not the fabulous things that your Brand Lovers care about, your promises are just meaningless noise.

Making promises requires keeping those promises. To maintain its market position, Shifu must continue to acquire the best beans and roast them to perfection. Operations must be calm, almost meditative—there are no harried baristas shouting orders at Shifu! The focus on tranquility is nonnegotiable. This is one of the brand's constants.

Messaging Strategy

The messaging strategy captures what the brand is saying, in terms of the words the customer actually hears. This may or may not be the business's tagline, but it definitely has a presence in all marketing and communication efforts.

What We Learned. Shifu's messaging strategy is: *inner peace and delight are only a mug of coffee away.*

Why This Is Important. By clearly articulating its messaging strategy, Shifu now has a baseline to come back to in all communication efforts. It doesn't matter what the medium is. Whether it's a roadside billboard, a radio advertisement, online marketing, or the philosophy guiding the barista as she prepares the perfect cup of Joe, the customer must hear one clearly articulated message.

Brand Identity

Brand identity is the aggregation of all the sensory information your Brand Lovers use to identify your organization. Much of Brand Identity is visual, focusing on colors, fonts, images, and iconography. Dominant organizations win by appealing to the eye and then taking it one step further.

At this point, we'll be examining the personality, imagery, sounds, and kinesthetics of the brand. For additional discussion of these topics, see Chapter 8.

Personality

If your brand were a person, what type of person would it be? People have an overwhelming, pervasive tendency to assign human qualities to totally inanimate objects. Corporations are no exception. It's not difficult to see Harley-Davidson embodied as a freedom-loving biker, clad in black leathers and grinning from ear to ear as the bike roars down the open road. Brand Lovers seek out organizations whose personality is most in alignment with their own.

What We Learned. If the Shifu brand were a person, it would be Keisuke Miyagi, the venerable karate master and kindly teacher from the *Karate Kid* movies. Mr. Miyagi is a master of his art, values calmness and contemplation, and is perpetually wise.

Why This Is Important. Understanding who the Shifu brand would be if it were a person provides a guide to how our best customers expect the Coffee Palace to act. Although it might seem trite to reduce this to "What would Mr. Miyagi do?," in many ways, that's exactly the type of question we should be asking. If a conflict or crisis comes up—a botched coffee order, a disruptive customer, or a sudden fluctuation in the world coffee market that causes prices to skyrocket—it is good to know that Brand Lovers expect a response worthy of Mr. Miyagi. It must be well thought out, delivered calmly, and show much wisdom.

Imagery

While words speak to our intellect, images communicate directly with our unconscious. As a result, images can play a vital role in connecting us quickly and compellingly to our best customers. It's essential that we seek out and identify the images that our Brand Lovers find most in keeping with their perceptions of the company's identity.

What We Learned. Researching Shifu's Brand Lovers, we learned that the following images resonate deeply: a flowing stream, a waterfall, misty mountains, bamboo, a Zen garden, stained hardwood, and rice paper.

Why This Is Important. Using images that resonate deeply with Shifu's Brand Lovers in marketing, advertising, and communication efforts, as well as within the Coffee Palace, will strengthen the bond that Shifu enjoys with its existing Brand Lovers. Additionally, strategic use of this imagery will help attract new people who find the images appealing. This can contribute to market share growth.

Knowing what works with absolute certainty eliminates the need to expend time, energy, and resources floundering around trying to pick something better. Proven results are hard to ignore. Using what works and continually refining that to make it more "on brand" introduces a beneficial element of organizational efficiency.

Sounds

The things that we hear are nearly as important as the things that we see. At this point, we focus on the sounds that Brand Lovers associate with your organization. Think of these sounds as a sort of auditory shorthand: when your Brand Lovers hear them, they think of you.

What We Learned. Much of Shifu's appeal is the sense of quiet retreat from the busy, noisy world. Yet the brand does not operate in total silence. Instead, there are four distinct, if unobtrusive, sounds that Brand Lovers have identified: moving water (streams, waterfalls, fountains, and so on), chirping birds, rustling trees, and coffee-brewing sounds.

Why This Is Important. These sounds play a vital role in the Shifu Brand Lover's experience. They enhance the enjoyment that the Brand Lover is already getting from drinking great coffee in a restful environment. It's essential not only that Shifu continue providing these sounds and looking for ways to successfully integrate them into customer touch points, as appropriate, but that it doesn't allow other sounds to become overwhelming and disruptive.

This means being particularly selective when considering expansion plans. A Shifu's Coffee Palace located in a busy airport, for example, might seem like a good idea: there are few times that a peaceful retreat is as welcome as when you've got a four-hour layover in a strange city. However, it may be nearly impossible to get the quiet space needed, given the steady dull roar of ambient noise that's part and parcel of a busy airport.

Kinesthetics

Kinesthetics refer to the tactile experience that your brand offers. Texture and feel are subtle considerations that are seldom articulated, yet are hugely important.

What We Learned. Researching Shifu's Brand Lovers revealed that they associated the following textures or surfaces with the company: wood, soft and smooth, and warm.

Why This Is Important. Integrating the feel of wood, or of surfaces that are soft and smooth, into the Coffee Palace environment is essential. Any planned expansion must include these vital tactile elements.

Ambient temperature is also an important consideration. Shifu's Brand Lovers associate feeling warm, a sensation that they find welcoming and nurturing, with the company. That's important to remember. Too much air conditioning can make Shifu's Brand Lovers order that coffee to go—even if they're not sure why.

Brand Vision

At the end of the Brand Modeling process, we integrate all of the information gathered throughout the process into a comprehensive Brand Vision. This vision is the ultimate tool for making decisions that affect your business.

The Brand Vision articulates what your company needs in order to succeed. When you're performing in alignment with your Brand Vision, you'll find the ranks of your Brand Lovers growing. Your market share will increase, and your profitability will grow.

All decisions, including those faced by Mr. Shifu, can be viewed through the lens of the Brand Vision. If a campaign, say the West Coast expansion, can be undertaken in a way that is in alignment with the principles outlined in the Brand Vision, it is a good decision. Weighing all options—including the franchise plan and the drive to get Shifu coffee beans into a retail setting—against the same criteria allows leaders to make apples-to-apples comparisons. It may be that Shifu's leadership is facing three good choices. But only Brand Modeling will reveal whether all of the choices are equally good, and which has the possibility for the greatest rewards.

In this section, we look at Brand Lover characteristics, company perceptions, customer perceptions, and emotional targets. For further discussion, please see Chapter 9.

Brand Lover Characteristics

At this point, we want the definitive set of characteristics that best describe your Brand Lovers. These characteristics are the terms that your Brand Lovers would use to describe themselves.

What We Learned. Researching Shifu's Brand Lovers, we discovered the following quartet of customer characteristics: intellectually oriented, aesthetically inclined, seeker, and calm.

Why This Is Important. Many dominant organizations win because they offer their best customers a sense of community. Their Brand Lovers feel like they belong. Shifu will succeed by continuing to offer an environment and an experience designed to appeal to the intellectually oriented, aesthetically inclined, and calm seeker. Messaging should be designed to resonate with this audience. These are the Brand Lovers who will take Shifu to the next level.

Company Perceptions

The company perceptions are the internal component of Brand Vision. This is how the organization sees itself, including an articulation of values that are important to leaders and frontline workers alike.

What We Learned. Shifu sees itself as being committed to the art of coffee, operating with the highest standards, welcoming, and ecologically conscious.

Why This Is Important. Clearly articulating your company's internal values is essential for two reasons. First, today's customers value transparency; they want to know what guides the organizations they do business with, and they monitor how closely a company adheres to its own values. Second, company perception is critical in helping to create an organization-wide unity of vision, which is essential for brand dominance.

Customer Perceptions

Customer perceptions are the distilled essence of everything the Brand Lover thinks about the company. We're looking for the three or four main commonly held beliefs.

What We Learned. Shifu's Brand Lovers see the company as being serene, high quality, artistic, and inviting.

Why This Is Important. Customer perceptions are customer expectations. Every encounter that Shifu's customers have with the brand is judged against these criteria. Was the setting serene? Was the coffee exceptionally good? Were the baristas helpful and understanding of special requests? Was the entire experience one of a kind? This isn't a wish list; these are baseline expectations. This is the standard that must be met or exceeded if Shifu is to triumph.

Emotional Targets

We finish where we started, by identifying the emotional targets that our Brand Lovers are seeking when they do business with us. Brand dominance is no more complicated than consistently hitting these emotional targets better than anyone else in the marketplace. It helps to know what those targets are.

What We Learned. Shifu's emotional targets are awe, peacefulness, connectedness, and comfort.

Why This Is Important. We know that the emotional appeal of Shifu's brand is awe, peacefulness, connectedness, and comfort. Every single customer touch point should strive to hit one or more of these emotional targets. The more Shifu's can evoke these emotions in its customers, the more equity the brand will gain.

Brand Vision Statement

To summarize, Shifu's Brand Vision statement says:

> *Especially for the intellectually oriented, aesthetically inclined, and calm seeker, Shifu's Coffee Palace is the ecologically conscious, welcoming coffee shop with a commitment to the art of coffee and maintaining the highest standards. As a unique, accommodating, serene environment with the highest-quality coffee, Shifu's provides its customers with a sense of awe, peacefulness, connectedness, and comfort.*

IMPLEMENTING THE MODEL

Armed with the Brand Model, Mr. Shifu, Ms. Koh, and the rest of the Shifu leadership team can assess potential expansion plans more critically and effectively.

The Brand Lovers' emphasis on the quiet, serene, and individual nature of the Shifu's experience does not preclude expansion. It does, however, make clear the need to be extremely selective about location and staffing choices. Pinpointing those neighborhoods that would value a quiet, meditative coffee shop is fundamentally different from figuring out where to plunk down the next drive-through doughnut shop. The time and effort that go into this more cautious approach are more than amply rewarded when a shop opens in exactly the right location, one where customers rave about how long "this town" has needed "something like this."

With this in mind, Shifu's has decided to move forward cautiously with the West Coast expansion, growing only in those locations where it can reliably deliver the serene experience and high-quality coffee drinks that it is known for. Locations that are not conducive to the Zen-like feel of Shifu's are rejected summarily. This does not mean that the locations identified were not good locations. They may in fact be highly profitable for other companies, but they will not work for Shifu's.

After more investigation, it was determined that the ability to ensure the superior experience that Shifu is known for and that its Brand Lovers cherish above all else would be extremely difficult to guarantee through a franchise plan. Rather than imperil the relationship Shifu has with its existing Brand Lovers, the franchise plan was shelved.

Ms. Koh's plans to get Shifu-branded beans into a retail setting took a slightly different track from the one she had initially envisioned. After realizing the value that Shifu's Brand Lovers placed on unique, peaceful experiences, Shifu decided to move forward with the retail initiative, but only in those gourmet boutiques and specialty stores that consistently deliver a shopping experience that would appeal to Shifu's Brand Lovers. Shifu's customers have both the disposable income and the inclination to patronize specialty grocery stores, whereas the typical "shop and save" customer is unlikely to fully appreciate Shifu's products or approach.

The retail initiative was successful because Shifu followed its Brand Lovers into the retail marketplace. It pursued placement in the stores that its Brand Lovers already frequented. This approach eliminated much of the expense and logistics involved with major grocery placement, yet delivered consistently strong sales. Shifu-branded beans became a profitable revenue stream for the company.

Brand Modeling provided Shifu with a safe, reliable way to predict the outcome of several major initiatives with a high degree of certainty. Providing the leadership team with reliable, actionable intelligence facilitated smart, strategic decision making.

Shifu's enjoyed the benefits of this smart decision making. It increased its brand visibility, market share, and organizational profitability. And they did it all by putting customers first.

For suggested reading and more information on
Brand Modeling, visit www.Brand-Modeling.com.

Index

215

A New Growth Strategy
for the World's Leading Brands

B rand Modeling offers a powerful growth strategy that has been proven to work in both up and down markets. If it is implemented throughout an organization, its results will speak for themselves.

Large companies spend millions on advertising and marketing efforts without having a means of maximizing their effects, with the result that these efforts often simply irritate customers or are just not relevant to them—even though the companies have conducted market research. Brand Modeling solves this industrywide problem, offering unprecedented clarity and strategic focus, and improving the return on investment of future initiatives by more than 300 percent.

Brand Modeling helps business leaders—especially CEOs and CMOs—stay focused on the big picture, making effective decision-making possible through more accurate, statistically verifiable data and insights. It offers a radical departure from "business as usual," providing innovating thinkers with new perspectives on how to grow more profitable—and sustainable—businesses by focusing on the driving force behind any business: its best customers.

Brand Modeling helps marketers develop effective go-to-market strategies that have an impact on the business's position in the industry, offering unprecedented differentiation and market share growth.

About The Cult Branding Company

For more than a decade, The Cult Branding Company has dedicated itself to studying what makes brands like Apple, Harley-Davidson, Southwest Airlines, and IKEA so successful and how they build undeniable customer loyalty and cultlike followings while their competitors flounder.

Although not every business can develop into a Cult Brand, every business has Brand Lovers—loyal, profitable customers that buy its brand with greater frequency and provide positive word of mouth.

Led by Bolivar J. Bueno, the Cult Branding team has been developing and refining a process to uncover and decode a brand's best customers.

Using depth analysis, humanistic psychology, and comparative mythology, the team has innovated a means of unveiling the psychological and behavioral drivers behind customer motivation.

Using these customer insights, generated through proprietary psychological assessments, in-depth interviews, and sophisticated competitive study, the Cult Branding team deploys rigorous statistical analysis to develop comprehensive models for some of today's most successful brands, including Kohl's Department Stores, Turner Classic Movies, Scheels, TradeStation Securities, the LA Lakers, and The Life is good Company.

**Visit The Cult Branding Company at
www.cultbranding.com**

**Subscribe to our weekly blog for fresh
perspectives on Brand Modeling:
www.brand-modeling.com**